DATE DUE			

CLASSICAL DANCE

JANE ROBBINS

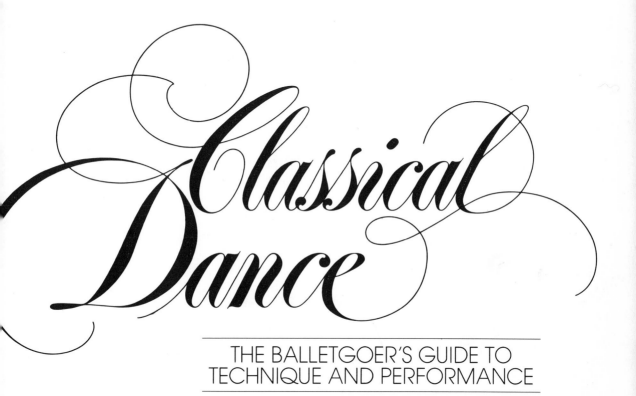

Classical Dance

THE BALLETGOER'S GUIDE TO TECHNIQUE AND PERFORMANCE

HOLT, RINEHART AND WINSTON
New York

Published by Holt, Rinehart and Winston, 383 Madison Avenue,
New York, New York 10017.
Published simultaneously in Canada by Holt, Rinehart and Winston
of Canada, Limited.

Library of Congress Cataloging in Publication Data
Robbins, Jane, 1948–
Classical Dance: The balletgoer's guide to technique and performance
1.   Ballet dancing.   I.   Title.
GV1788.R6   792.8   80-24735
ISBN: 0-03-048941-5

First Edition

Designer: Joy Chu
Printed in the United States of America
1 3 5 7 9 10 8 6 4 2

TO BOB,
EVER GENEROUS AND UNQUESTIONING

Contents

Preface   ix
Acknowledgments   xiii
A Note to the Reader   xv

PLACEMENT

1 Posture and Muscle Control   5
2 The Legs and Feet   12
3 The Arms   24
4 Positions of the Body/*Épaulement*   33
5 *Pointe* Work and Partnering   50

MOVEMENT

6 Jumps and Beats   69

7 Turns   85

8 Linking Movements   96

DANCE

9 Choreography   105

10 The Dynamics of Performance   113

ENCORES

The Training   123

The Ballet Tradition   131

Looking Backward: Evolution of the Art and Technique of Ballet   175

Index   183

PREFACE

When I was little I never wanted to be a ballerina. It didn't occur to me that people danced to earn a living; indeed, at that age I don't think it occurred to me that people had to work at anything at all. Ballet dancers to me were not real creatures. I recall sometimes going to a big place, a very exciting place, where you sat in a seat that scratched your legs, and you looked up at an enormously high ceiling until the lights went out. Then suddenly, far away, a spot of light would appear in which visions in the prettiest colored dresses floated and flew around; it was like spying on fairies through a drainpipe in some dark, silent wood. Then they would disappear, it would become very bright again, and we would go home. That was all.

It seems odd to me now, as I write a book whose chief aim is to foster appreciation for the qualities and abilities that make ballet dancers such an elite group of professionals, that I ever had so casual an attitude about ballet dancers, and that it could have persisted so far into adulthood. Of course I took ballet les-

sons when I was a child—everyone did then, and they still do. But classes in a small town in New Jersey in the fifties did not, as a rule, constitute good training, and ballet then was not as universally popular and highly regarded as it is today. I quit ballet early and seriously pursued other kinds of dancing, with professional training, for many years. I was well into my twenties before I decided to take ballet lessons again, and I went into it with the attitude that it would be easy, for surely all dancing was the same.

One class set me straight—with all the stinging surprise of a slap in the face and the bewilderment of being roused from a dream. Here I was, a professionally trained modern dancer, dripping wet, frighteningly weak and shaky, blindingly light-headed, at the end of an intermediate-level class—a class that was much too difficult for me but that somehow I had followed and completed. It was the beginning of a long, slow (and continuing) education.

Though the school of hard knocks is undoubtedly an effective way to learn about things, there are other successful methods. Reading, for example, can be so instructive—and so much more pleasant. For all who enjoy the beautiful art of ballet and would like to know more about the dancing—but who lack the time, inclination, or fanaticism necessary to learn about it firsthand—I have put some of what I have learned into this book. It is not a substitute for going to the ballet, of course; if you are serious about learning about ballet, you should go as much as you can, seeing whatever and whoever is available. It is, instead, a primer and reference book that can prepare you, introduce to you, explain to you, illustrate for you, or refresh your memory according to your changing needs.

As you read, you will notice that I am always talking about the *qualities* that specific dancers, movements, and aspects of the technique have, and how they contribute to the art of ballet dancing as a whole. Classical ballet is a precise—almost scientific—highly refined, *complete* technique. Nothing—not a single nuance of movement or position—has been neglected in its delineation. Classical ballet technique is really a body of knowledge, not a mere battery of steps, and classical dancers are its scholars. Realizing the brilliance, the balance, and the subtlety of the technique, and seeing the blending and perfection of its infinite qualities, make going to the ballet unendingly fresh, stimulating, and enjoyable. I hope this book will help you love it as much as I do.

JANE ROBBINS

ACKNOWLEDGMENTS

I would like to thank my dancer, Edra Toth, of Boston Repertory Ballet, and my photographer, Michael Malyszko, whose professionalism, cooperation, dedication, technical mastery, and humor and enthusiasm enabled me to develop a concept into the stunning and instructive photographs in this book.

I am also grateful to Sam Kurkjian, director of Boston Repertory Ballet, for discussions that contributed substantially to the chapters on choreography and performance, and for the use of his studio; and to Milou Ivanovsky, whose ideas formed the basis of the chapter on linking movements. Talks with other friends and former teachers influenced the text in less identifiable yet still valuable ways. I would particularly like to thank Leo Guerard, ballet master of Boston Repertory Ballet; Kira Ivanovsky, director of Ballet Fantasque; and Herci Marsden, director of Rhode Island State Ballet, for the time and thought they gave to answering my questions.

xiii

Special thanks to my typist, Sue Dunham, and to Judy Hughes and Kennet Oberley, whose cheerful contributions defy narrow description. And finally, thanks to all the people who worked on the publication of this book: Peter Skolnik, Natalie Chapman, Joy Chu, Catherine Killeffer, and Tricia West.

A NOTE TO THE READER

This book is about *classical* ballet in that it discusses technique as it is taught in the schools. Classical technique is the foundation for all ballet, and all good ballet is based on classical principles and the classical vocabulary. What you see at the ballet, however, need not be a perfect reflection or application of what is described here. Ballet, like art and music, uses its academic foundation and repertory of classical works as a guide and means to new creative achievements. In contemporary choreography, dancers may move in ways that are not strictly classical—that may, in fact, be unorthodox. Always look for the classical basis of movement, or its natural evolution from and consistency with academic technique: if it is there, the movement is legitimate.

Throughout the book, a dancer is referred to as "he" or "she" depending on what seemed most natural or appropriate for the topic being discussed rather than according to any hard rules.

To the extent possible, the fundamentals of ballet placement and movement discussed in the text are illustrated in the photographs. Most photographs immediately follow the relevant discussion, but it may be necessary to flip ahead to find them. They will help you understand and visualize what is being talked about in the text.

Placement

Placement is the positioning of the arms, the legs, and the body, shoulders, and head in relation to each other and to the basic posture. An acceptable definition, but one that scarcely communicates the vast importance that *placement,* an otherwise inconsequential little word, assumes when uttered in reference to ballet. Indeed, preceded by the word "good" or "bad," it can sum up a dancer's chances for a successful career. It can say whether she possesses "line"—the indispensable quality of presenting a beautiful outline to the audience in all poses and movements. It can say whether she will ever be able to do multiple turns with one leg extended out to the side and, in fact, whether she will ever be able to turn properly at all. It can be the reason that she is unable to hold a balance on *pointe,* or that her partner looks terrible while he stands and supports her. It says, in short, almost everything about the basic technique of the dancer. That is why placement is the focus of the training for the first several years, and the focus of half the chapters of this book.

POSTURE AND
MUSCLE CONTROL

efore a child can walk—and certainly before he can run, jump, or balance on a fence rail—he must learn to stand and to control the muscles that will move him the way he wants. Before a dancer can walk like a dancer—or run, or jump, or balance like a dancer—he too must first learn to stand and control his muscles.

Most of us take standing erect and moving in complicated ways for granted, so it is hard to think of dancers, of all people, as having to learn correct posture and muscle control. But dancers' movements are different from ours. Their running, jumping, and balancing are done to the extremes of precision, complexity, and difficulty. They do even the most commonplace movement—walking, for example—in an exceptional way. The difference is not so much in kind as in degree, and the same is true of their posture and muscle control: they are not so

different from ours (that is, if ours are reasonably good), but they are much more exact and highly developed.

These qualities are not obvious to us. We may notice how very regal and graceful a dancer is when just standing or walking, or be amazed at how she can dance long, demanding roles seemingly effortlessly, but we don't really see the intricate workings of the body that enable her to do it.

The dancer's posture is one reason we are never aware of any strain or tension or forcefulness in a dancer's movements. It is very natural and relaxed-looking—graceful and ethereal, yet somehow still stately and strong.

When the dancer is at rest, her chin is level and her gaze steady and straight ahead. The body, from the feet to the head, is pulled up and carried tall, with every muscle elongated. The neck is long and the shoulders are down, relaxed, and square with the hips. It is extremely important, not only to the dancer's grace and line, but to her ability to turn, jump, and balance, that the shoulders be down and square, and never hunched, twisted, pulled back, or rounded. The arms are soft, rounded down to the fingertips with elbows uplifted, and held slightly away from the body. The chest is open, expansive, with the diaphragm held high and the abdomen in. The entire torso is centered over the legs, which, as we will talk about in the next chapter, are well turned out from the hips and evenly placed over the feet. When the torso is properly centered, the pelvis also is centered, and we see, when the dancer is in profile, the slight natural curve of the spine. If the pelvis is tipped forward, the dancer looks swaybacked, with a deep arch, and the legs exert too much pressure on the inside of the foot, forcing the feet to "roll over" and the head to strain back. If the pelvis is tipped backward, the dancer is "tucked under": her spine flattens, losing its natural curve, her legs are forced back so that she is "sitting" a little on her heels, and her neck and head are thrown forward and slightly downward.

Despite the fact that the dancer must be unrelenting about "pulling up," the position is soft and easy—nothing like that of the soldier at attention, with his

1. The elegant, controlled-but-at-ease posture of the dancer, with the torso directly centered over the legs. The openness from across the chest down through the rounded arms, and the elongation of the body from head to foot, combine to give an impression of commanding nobility.

chin thrust up and out, his shoulders pulled severely back, his breast protruding like a chicken's, and his rear end sticking out. Though the description is almost a caricature, it suits the pose many people strike when assuming the stance of a dancer, and illustrates, by contrast, exactly what the dancer's posture is not.

Absolute control of the muscles enables the dancer to maintain her posture. When a dancer holds herself completely drawn up, the muscles of the torso are like an accordion being held open; when she doesn't, the muscles sag, like an accordion that has been let go.

The torso is in fact the center of muscle control in the dancer, for it is the muscles of the abdomen, buttocks, and lower back or waist—along with the muscles of the thighs—that supply the stability, force, and holding power to execute ballet's difficult movements (particularly jumps) and to sustain poses. In general, all movements are accomplished by the concerted tightening (or, more precisely, a total stretching that results in a taut muscle) and strength of these four muscle groups. For example, in the *arabesque* position, where the dancer stands on one leg with the other extended behind, the thigh muscles are used to raise the leg to an unnatural height, the lower back and buttock muscles hold the leg in position, the buttock and abdomen muscles maintain the balance, and the back muscles hold the body erect and still. The upper body is left free of tension, enabling the dancer to move the head and arms gracefully and make even the most strenuous movement appear to be performed with ease.

In a balance, the entire sustaining power is in the torso and thighs. The dancer draws herself way up out of the hips so that she feels the pull all along the face of the leg, under the buttocks, up through the stomach, and particularly up through the sides and the spine. Any tendency to let go a little at the waist on the side of the supporting leg not only makes the balance look terrible—pinched and off-center—but also significantly reduces the length of time it can be held. Control of the muscles is so important for balances that in practicing them at the *barre*, the student is admonished over and over again, "Don't think of balancing; think of *pulling up*."

One of the most remarkable things about a dancer's mastery over her muscles is that she is able to direct not only groups of muscles, but single muscles in isolation. Many movements and positions in ballet depend on this ability, which springs from the intuitive, highly specialized anatomical knowledge acquired through years of working with one's body. The use of "pull and counterpull" of various muscles, for example, is fundamental to virtually everything a dancer does, particularly sustained movements and poses. To stand in *arabesque* on the right leg, the dancer stretches the left leg well behind, but simultaneously exerts a forward pressure, or pull, in the left hip to prevent it from twisting back with the leg and to keep it squarely in line with the other hip. To stand in *passé*, a position on one leg with the other raised and bent in to form a triangle with the foot at the knee, the muscles of the thighs pull up to lift the leg, while the muscles of the hip and buttocks push down to prevent the hip from rising up out of line and to help keep the body from leaning toward the standing leg. Even the movements of the arms rely on pull and counterpull for correct execution. While the muscles of the upper arm lift it overhead, the muscles in the shoulders and shoulder blades simultaneously pull down to keep them always open and unhunched. The beautiful winglike beating movement of the arms in *Swan Lake* is completely dependent on this precise manipulation of the arm and shoulder muscles.

While the dancer must be able to tighten and hold the muscles, she must also be able to relax them instantaneously, even if for only a second. For example, we sometimes see a ballerina do a seemingly endless series of turns, going up-down, up-down on *pointe*. How does she do it? Well, she possesses great strength and stamina, certainly, but she also "rests" each time she lowers her foot to prepare for the next turn. As her heel touches the floor and she bends her

knee, she relaxes her muscles for a split second, sinking softly into the movement. The tightening, relaxing, tightening action is second nature, almost invol-
untary; there is no time to think about it, and we in the audience are not even
aware it is occurring. It is subtle, but without it the dancer could never keep up
the constant flow of jumps, turns, balances, and quick little steps and beats of
the feet. And her movements would lack their soft quality.

Although correct posture and muscle control become an intrinsic part of a
dancer and are the first thing taught, it is a long, long time before they are spon-
taneous. At the beginning, and indeed almost throughout her training, a dancer
must consciously work on them. Even professionals, who must place and control
themselves automatically during a performance, continue to work at posture and
muscle control in the classes that they never stop taking: checking the hips to be
sure they are level and square, trying to increase the duration of their balances
by consciously holding their stomachs and buttocks for as long as possible.

In class, the teacher can alert the student to a fault in her posture with the
merest touch of his hand. He circulates the room during the *barre* exercises,
lightly poking with his index finger the shoulder of one, the abdomen of another,
the back a few inches below the waist of another. Instantly, the shoulder goes
down, the stomach in and the chest up, the pelvis back to the center. If the upper body is sagging—and it's surprising, how even when you think you're as
pulled up as possible, it still sags—the teacher may draw the body up tall with
a stroking and gentle pressure that is like a potter at his wheel pulling, by the
repeated upward strokes of his flat palms, a tall, graceful cylinder out of a form-
less lump of clay. The teacher places one palm on the abdomen, the other on
the back below the waist, and smooths the body up through the back and chest
in two or three quick strokes. It is such an effective little trick that students can
often be seen testing and adjusting themselves at the *barre* in the same way.

The teaching and correction of muscle control is, necessarily, almost entirely
verbal: no one can tighten your muscles for you. Good teachers, however, have

a keen eye for the body and an impressive knowledge of which little muscles and tendons do what. Possessed of these attributes, they have for hundreds of years successfully taught control by the simple but effective technique of yelling in the students' ears. While the class dances the combination of movements the teacher has given, the teacher shouts over the music, "Don't kick the leg, *lift* it! Use the muscles inside your thigh! Don't let the stomach go; that's why you're losing the balance. Now, *entrechat*, hold the back, stretch the thighs. Stronger back; you can't jerk the body like that!" And so on. It's a kind of prodding, a pushing you to do more, work harder. And there's always a little irritation in the voice; after all, the students know this already, and a ballet student must be able to work herself hard.

There comes a time, however, when the screaming, and the poking and re-adjusting, must come to an end. There will always be an occasional correction in a class or after rehearsal, surely, but a dancer must take her posture naturally and the muscles must work automatically. The sooner she arrives at this point, the better; she can go on to learn ballet's difficult jumps and turns with greater ease than those who are still sagging and bending and hunching. And, as I once heard a teacher say to a promising but somewhat lazy student, "Yes, you do beautifully when I yell. But there is no one to yell at you onstage. You are on your own."

THE LEGS AND FEET

$\mathcal{P}$roper posture and muscle control leave the legs and feet free to do their work—and work they must. They move the body through its myriad steps and poses; turn, balance, and support it; raise and lower it in *pointe* work; propel it into the air; and absorb the shock when it lands. Obviously, the legs and feet must be strong and flexible. But strength and flexibility, even though uncommon strength and flexibility, are not enough. For a dancer to execute steps with speed, precision, and clarity, to form a design in the air when he jumps or a pattern on the floor when he moves, to turn with alacrity and to balance without hesitation, and always to present a good line to the audience, his legs and feet must also be correctly placed. The legs must be well turned out, and the feet must proceed through or hold one of the five "school" positions in all movements.

It is impossible to talk about anything having to do with the legs and feet in ballet without first talking about turnout, because turnout is at the essence of all

their movements. It is the hallmark of classical dancing, the one thing more than any other that distinguishes it from all other forms of dance. Without at least some understanding of what it is we can never fully appreciate a dancer's astounding abilities.

Unfortunately, turnout is an extremely difficult concept to explain, and still more difficult to understand unless one has felt it. Maybe combining strict definition with an explanation of what it looks like to us in the audience, what it does for the dancer, and how it works anatomically will give you a sense of what turnout is.

Turnout is a 90-degree rotation of the leg bone in the hip socket from its normal position outward, such that a dancer facing the audience and pointing one leg forward will exhibit the inside of the extended leg—rather than the front— in a sort of profile. Similarly, a dancer standing in profile with the leg closer to the audience extended (front, side, or back) will exhibit the front of the leg to the audience when the leg is properly turned out.

Although the effect is visually pleasing, it was not for aesthetic reasons that turnout was developed; aesthetics were only a bonus. Turnout accomplishes something for the dancer: it enables him to do more than he otherwise could. Pure hip movement—the movement of the leg in its normal state without bringing other parts of the body (e.g., the spine) into play—is limited to about 60 degrees forward, 40 degrees side, and only 15 degrees back.* You can see this yourself by standing with your feet together and then slowly raising one leg as high as you can front, side, and back. What happens is really very simple. When you raise the leg, the knobby end of the big upper thighbone hits the edge of its socket, and further movement is impossible. Also limiting movement, especially to the back, is a large ligament across the front of the joint.

This leaves the dancer with somewhat of a problem. Classical technique today

*C. Sparger, *Anatomy and Ballet* (London: Adam and Charles Black, 1949).

demands that the dancer be able to extend the leg forward to *at least* 100 degrees, sideways to at least 135 degrees, and backward to at least 90 degrees (without substantially leaning over). So he turns out, coupling that movement with a pulling way up out of the hips and sometimes an adjustment in the spine or pelvis. He is thereby able to extend the leg higher and even to lift the ligament up over the impeding bone.

Turnout, then, gives the dancer greater freedom of movement in all directions; it gives the legs more play. It has other benefits as well. By providing a greater surface area over which the body is centered, it increases the dancer's stability. (Try swaying from side to side while standing with your heels together and your toes turned out; and then try the same thing with your feet straight together in their natural position; your balance and axial movement are greater in the former position because your weight is distributed over a greater area.) Turnout facilitates turns because a leg that is well turned out in a turn will lead or pull the body around, giving it direction. Turns like *tour à la seconde*, in which the dancer holds one leg extended to the side at a height of 90 degrees, would be impossible if the leg were not fully turned out from the hip; a turned-in leg would hold the dancer back and make the turn sluggish.

There is an aesthetic point worth noting here also. In ballet, all movement is done to the direction in which the leg is pointing; the feet are like arrows, and they land in the spot where they are aimed. This is one of the things that makes ballet a continuous flow, that makes it smooth and pleasing, and gives us a sense of expansive, open movement, even when a dance is done within a very small circumference. If the legs and feet were not always distinctly turned out, the uplifted knee would seem to lag behind the rest of the body in *pirouettes*; a turned-in foot would seem to be going against the direction of the rest of the leg. The sense of energy and forward movement in ballet dancing would be lost.

Finally, it is probably worth qualifying what I mean by well turned out. Ninety-degree turnout is a theoretical ideal that few (if any) dancers possess:

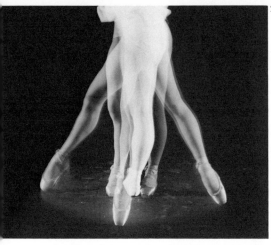

2 and 3. Turnout from the hip down through the foot, enabling free rotary movement of the leg in the hip joint, is developed in part through the *barre* exercise *rond de jambe à terre* (left). In this picture, the dancer begins from a tight, turned-out fifth position with the left leg front. Always pressing the heel well forward to help maintain the turnout from the hip, she brushes the front leg forward along the floor, stretching the foot; glides it around to the side and to the back; and then brushes it back into a flat, tight fifth position to complete the semicircular movement. Because only the left leg moves—with the standing leg and the torso from the hips up remaining immobile and squarely front—this exercise also develops the stability in a turned-out position the dancer needs to execute movements out on the floor.

Rond de jambe is also done *en l'air* (''in the air''), both at the *barre* as an exercise and as a dance movement, usually either with a *relevé* or a little jump off the standing leg. You can see from the picture (below) that, as the leg delineates an oval in the air, virtually all the

action is from the knee down, and the body stands motionless. This has the added benefit of developing strength in the thigh while developing stability, turnout in the hips, and pliancy in the lower leg.

though in certain stationary positions it may be possible to come very close, it is virtually impossible to maintain an extremely turned out position *in both legs* throughout the dance. The degree of turnout possible also varies markedly from dancer to dancer; turnout is more easily developed in certain body types than in others, and to a greater extent. The fact is that both someone with close to a 90-degree turnout and someone with, say, 75-degree turnout when standing in first position can be said to have good turnout if their turnout is correct; beyond a certain minimum, it is more a matter of quality than of degree.

Correctness in turnout implies that the turnout is from the hip and extends down through the feet; the feet alone do not (or should not) turn out. If the face of the knee (what appears as the kneecap) is centered over the entire area of the foot, the entire leg is turned out. But if the knee "remains behind" when the foot is turned out, it will appear to be twisted in and, at most, on a line with only the big toe or inside ankle. This stance, even though the feet may appear to be perfectly turned out, is not true turnout, and is useless and damaging to the dancer. Almost invariably the posture will be thrown off and the weight of the body thrust too far forward, causing a "rolling over" onto the inside of the foot, a lack of stability, and, in general, an ugly appearance (to say nothing of the wearing and abrasion to the knee joint). When lifted off the floor, the leg will involuntarily turn in altogether, the lower leg "giving in" to the inward pressure of the upper.

The dancer tries to maintain as good turnout in the legs as possible when standing on both legs; when standing on one leg, the working leg (the one in the air or off the floor) is turned out to the maximum extent possible while turnout in the supporting leg is adjusted slightly to permit smooth, steady execution of the movement. The turned-out foot is an extension of the leg. It is not just a matter of pointing; a pointed foot can be "sickled" (curved) out or in by an incorrect stretching of the muscles on either side below the ankle. Once again, the foot follows the entire line of the leg so that the furthermost point of the toes aligns with the knee, so what we see from the audience when the foot is pointed toward us is a foot stretched but not the least bit cramped or twisted-looking, with a beautiful curve and the heel visible as the dancer presses it well forward for maximum turnout. The sole of the foot is nowhere in sight.

Turnout is at the foundation of the five positions of the feet: *first* position, in which the feet, heels touching, form a straight line perpendicular to the body; *second*, in which the feet similarly form a straight line but with a space of about a foot between them; *third*, in which the feet are placed horizontally one in front of the other, each heel at about the midpoint of the other foot; *fourth*, in which the feet are aligned as in third position but there is a space of about a foot between them; and *fifth*, in which the feet are fully horizontal one in front of the other so that the heel of each touches the big toe of the other. In all positions the knees are straight and the weight is centered over the feet so that the feet are firmly and evenly placed on the floor; the heel, the big toe, and the little toe, forming a sort of triangle, should be under equal pressure. If the big toe or the little toe is taking too much weight, the feet roll in or out, respectively; if the heel takes too much, the dancer is "sitting" on the heels, and he appears tucked under. Good, pulled-up posture and turnout are necessary to avoid these problems.

A dancer cannot learn anything else until he has learned these five positions, and cannot do any step well unless he is master of them. Their importance is readily related: every step and movement in ballet begins and ends in one of the five classical positions, and many movements are by definition progressions through two or more positions. Even while a dancer hovers in the air at the height of a big jump, his position is defined by one of the five positions of the feet; never do they simply dangle.

For many movements, the correct position is more than just a way to begin; it is a *preparation* without which the dancer could not do the movement. This is true, for example, of all kinds of turns. The dancer must begin with his feet precisely placed in one of the five positions (and with his body precisely placed)

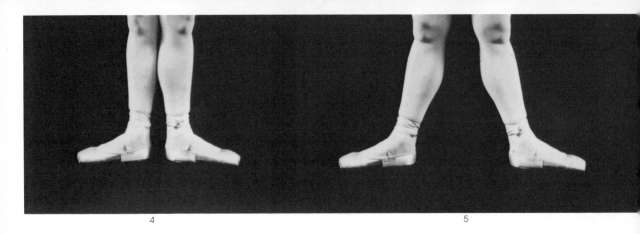

4

5

4-9. The five school positions of the feet are fundamental to all movements in ballet, so the dancer must learn to assume them naturally and precisely. Though all are important, none is so critical to the classical technique as a close and secure but easily placed fifth—the position that begins and ends countless jumps, poses, turns, and linking movements in the dance. (Above, from left: first, second, third, fourth, and fifth. The full view of fifth, right, shows the turnout from the hip, with the knees straight and over the feet.)

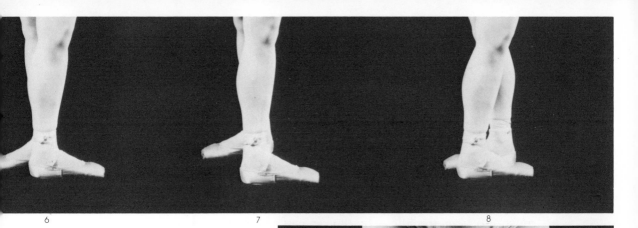

6   7   8

9

or he will never turn without falling over. If, for example, he is going to turn from a fourth-position preparation and the space between his feet is a little too wide or too narrow, or the back foot is under- or overcrossed with the front foot, the turn will never come off.

Implicitly, of course, the placement of the feet cannot be merely precise, it must also be automatic. The dancer can't be looking down to see if his feet are aligned or properly spaced, and moving them around until they are just so. For one thing, there is no time, and for another, it would look awful. Even slight adjustments would be noticeable to the audience, and would thereby thwart one of ballet's chief aims—to present a continuous flow of movement.

Precise positions of the feet are also probably the single most important element in making all movements—even at fast tempos—sharp, clean, and distinctive. They give a smart finish to jumps and turns, and give beats and midair poses their clarity and brilliance. They are particularly crucial in combinations of running, walking, and gliding steps along the floor; without them, the steps would muddy together like so many watercolors on a wet paper. They are the enunciations of dance, preventing dance sentences from becoming unintelligibly slurred. Indeed, a dancer with a correct, tight, comfortable fifth position—the hardest and at the same time the most recurring position in ballet—possesses an important quality for ballet.

Always keeping in mind that everything in classical ballet is done with the legs and feet turned out and in the five positions, we can now talk a little about strength and stretch. In ballet, the muscles of the legs and feet must be developed to possess a perfect balance between strength and stretch. This is in contrast to most physical activities, in which the ability to perform primarily depends more on one than another (e.g., football and baseball depend primarily on muscle strength; long-distance running and swimming depend primarily on muscle length).

The strength of the leg muscles gives the dancer the holding power for maintaining the leg in positions in the air, for lifting the leg slowly through the air to great heights without forcefully swinging it, and for supporting the body steadily through sustained periods of dancing. Much of this strength is concentrated in the thighs. Strong feet, particularly a strong instep and toes, supply the power for high jumps and rising onto *pointe*, and for working the feet in fast combinations of little jumps and beats without tiring.

Stretch in the leg muscles is essential for a good extension, or the ability to raise the leg to a point above the shoulder. Extension is the essence of the *développé*, the movement in which one leg is slowly unfolded from the floor up along the lower leg to the knee and then out to the front, side, or back at the highest possible point, to be held aloft for a moment. The *développé* is a mainstay of *adagio* (a dance in slow tempo), and as such means that a good extension is an absolute requirement for every classical dancer.

Stretch in the feet is probably most important of all, because it means so many things for the dancer. Flexible feet are responsive feet; devoid of stiffness, they can execute intricate combinations with sharpness and alacrity, and strong, thrusting movements with attack. They allow the dancer to go up and down through half-toe or full *pointe* smoothly. Fully stretched, they are beautiful to look at.

Flexibility in the feet is also essential for *demi-plié*, one of the structural underpinnings of ballet. *Demi-plié* is a deep bending of the knees in a very open (turned-out) position without lifting the heels off the floor, such that the flat foot and the lower leg form an acute angle. Although the action is in the knees, it is the feet that are most critical to the quality of a dancer's *demi-plié*. If he has by nature a very pliant Achilles tendon, he has been blessed with the capacity for *demi-plié*, and therefore has an advantage in many aspects of the dance. If he has not, he must develop one to the extent physically possible, for a dancer who lacks *demi-plié* (you see that it is so important as to be regarded as a quality in a dancer) will never look right and will never succeed as a professional.

10

11

10 and 11. The slow unfolding of the leg in the movement known as *développé* is a breathtaking display of a dancer's mastery of her body and her technique. From fifth position, the leg passes through three distinct positions before the final, held extension: *sur le cou-de-pied* ("on the neck of the foot"), *passé* (at the knee), and *attitude* (leg half-extended, with the knee bent). The arm and head move harmoniously with the leg through their own prescribed positions, as can more easily be seen in the picture on the right, where the fifth and attitude positions are not recorded. Distinctly visible in both pictures are the turnout; the constant stretch of the foot; the freedom of movement of the leg while the hips remain down and even; the relaxed, tension-free arms and upper body; and the extra bit of "lift" of the leg that the dancer achieves by breathing in at the last moment.

The reason is that *demi-plié* is intrinsic to all dance movements. As such, it plays both a functional and an artistic role: functional in that it provides impetus and elasticity for performing jumps, turns, and dances on *pointe* (see Chapters 5 through 7), and artistic in that it provides the qualities of plasticity and softness to the dance. The dancer who seems to float, whose movements are soft and springy and liquid, uses her *demi-plié* well.

Turnout, the positions of the feet, and the long, strong muscle are developed only by years of work at the *barre* repeating exercises that have been carefully designed to achieve the exact qualities desired in the legs and feet (see "The Training," pages 123–30). There are no shortcuts, and sloppiness or hurrying on to other aspects of the technique before it is time will only result in bad habits or bad qualities in the dancer. Sickled feet, rolling over, bulky calf muscles, turnout that does not originate at the hip, dangling feet, lack of differentiation in steps on the floor—all can be traced back to a period in the training when neither enough time nor enough attention was paid to the basics. So the training proceeds slowly; for the first year or so, for example, the student does very little else besides work on the five school positions and *demi-plié*. Turnout is acquired gradually, over the years. Exercises to develop strength and flexibility in the entire leg are added one by one and in increasing complexity as the student is ready. It is, after all, the basics that count, that make a dancer good. And it is *all* the basics, in combination; strength, or a high extension, or 90-degree turnout, or a pretty foot alone is insufficient. Next time you see a dancer do a *développé*, look beyond the high leg. Does she pull the leg up smoothly from a close fifth? Can she hold it there, steadily? Is her leg turned out and her foot well stretched, showing you a fine line? Is she standing very tall throughout and not all sunk in at the waist? If so, you are enjoying the distinct and all-too-elusive pleasure of watching a dancer who possesses many of the attributes of a fine technique.

THE ARMS

I once saw an old film of Maya Pliset-skaya of the Bolshoi Ballet in which she talked about the arms. The arms, she thought, were everything in the dance; they could say anything you wanted and make you anything you wanted to be. And the fingers spoke most of all. Watch, she said, I'll show you. And she just stood there and, moving nothing but her arms and her head, became first a Thai dancer, then a Russian peasant, then a tree, then a Spaniard, then a sorceress, then a bird, then a reindeer. She stood absolutely still, placed her arms angularly above her head, spread her fingers stiffly and unevenly, and she *was* a reindeer. Then she laughed and let her arms fall, and she was Plisetskaya again. It was quite remarkable—and very instructive.

At the ballet, one sees such magical transformations all the time, without realizing it. Next time you see *The Nutcracker*, for instance, notice how a hand on a hip and one flung overhead say "Spanish"; bent arms pulled in tight under

the chin with wriggling fingers say "creepy mouse"; stiff, jerky arms crooked at the elbows and palms held high say "mechanical doll." Almost the moment a dancer steps out on stage we know whether she is a witch or a princess, old or young, Russian or Spanish, a bird or a mouse. The arms speak, and communicate this to us.

The arms, by way of pantomime, can also tell us what is happening in a ballet. Though seldom used in contemporary choreography, pantomime is essential to most of the old full-length classics. In *The Sleeping Beauty*, for example, virtually the entire plot is communicated to the audience in gestures. The gestures of pantomime are simple—pointing, folding, or raising the hands in different ways—but they are expressive, familiar, and understandable to everyone.

The arms are not used only for storytelling or for character or demi-character dancing, however.* They are what finish and lend harmony to every step, and what in their infinite combination give uniqueness, style, distinction, to every move. In fact, one could even argue that it is the arms (and the body, as we will see in Chapter 4) that *make* the dance. In classical ballet, the feet stay in the school positions always. Every step, every jump or turn, is done in one or more of the five basic positions of the feet. The repertoire of steps, though always being put together differently, is also set and limited; choreographers are not forever coming up with new turns or jumps as are gymnasts or figure skaters. It is the arms that give variety to the dance and, more important, give it identity. Only the arms and hands can move freely, only the arms can *express*: not only character and age, but place, time, emotion, and mood.

It is fascinating to zero in on the arms for a few minutes during a ballet—to observe their constant changing of position, or their absolute suspended silence while the feet move wildly; the slowness or speed of their movement compared

---

* Character dancing is dancing that is characteristic of or native to a country—for example, a jig, polka, mazurka, or other "folk" dance. Demi-character is popular or folk dancing performed with some classical technique, perhaps on *pointe*. It is often used in portraying comic or easily stereotyped characters.

with the feet; their lightness in a forceful jump or turn; and their elegant stretch in an *arabesque*. The arms contribute immeasurably to what in ballet is called *line*, the outline presented as a result of the dancer's arrangement of the head, body, legs, and arms. Good line is developed slowly throughout the years of training; it is indispensable to the classical dancer, and it is impossible without good arms.

Good arms, however, are not quite so simple and natural as Plisetskaya makes them look. True, as with anything else in ballet, if you have a head start from nature—well-formed arms, with lovely skin and shoulders—you are in luck. But you will still need all the help you can get. The use of the arms in ballet is, as Vaganova, famous Russian dancer and teacher, once said, "a great science." *Port de bras*, the name for the series of exercises designed to make the arms move gracefully, independently, and harmoniously (and also for any movement of the arms from one position to another), is the foundation of that science—much as turnout is the foundation for all movements of the legs.

Many dance teachers would agree that the arms are the most difficult part of the technique to perfect. Any dance student will vouch for it, and bitterly if she has not yet mastered their control. Developing good technique in the use of the arms is so slow and complex, and demands so much concentration, that it is an almost perpetual study, and an almost perpetual target for correction. In every class the teacher can be seen circling the roomful of students at the *barre*, raising an elbow here, taking hold of a finger and gently jiggling the tension out of an arm there, pushing a hunched shoulder down, closing the fingers of a rigidly spread hand. Well-executed jumps or turns may be met with only the remark, "Your arms are too stiff." Good, stretched-out *arabesques* are frequently rewarded with, "Your arm is too high," or "Your shoulder is twisted; it looks awful." Combinations of movements may be repeated over and over until the arms, not just the feet, move through the dance correctly.

What's so hard? It certainly doesn't *look* hard, or even as if the movements

of the arms are "planned." But it's the old trick of rubbing your stomach and patting your head at the same time, although that's not an adequate example. It's more like being Seiji Ozawa conducting Beethoven's Fifth from the waist up and Fred Astaire dancing in *Carefree* from the waist down at the same time. The secret to the arms is perfect control over them, absolute mastery of their every move totally independent of anything else the body is doing. It's as if, through the training, a dancer develops two separately functioning brains: one for the legs and feet, one for the *port de bras*. And this is why the arms always look so un-choreographed, so effortless: they neither absorb nor reflect any of the tension from the rest of the body, and they need not parallel any directions or moves of the legs.

The proper position of the arms comes only when the strength and control of the legs is beginning to become second nature. When a student reaches a point at which every movement of the body is not a strain, then she can begin to hold the arms lightly, with no show of tension. It takes several years to learn just to *hold* the arms; it is much later that one begins to *move* them. For a long time the arms tend to "imitate" the movements of the legs by sharing in the work. For example, when a student does a *rond de jambe*, an exercise in which the pointed foot describes a circle on the floor, the arm unconsciously describes a vague circle in the air. Or when she does a *grand battement*, in which the arm is often held up over the head in third position, the arm often "kicks back" jerk-ily as the leg is kicked high. So during the long time a student works on the basic development of the legs, little more is required of the arms than that they remain still and be held in the correct position. This in itself requires great effort and concentration.

In the correct position, the shoulder is down and relaxed, the elbow is held up, never drooping, and the entire arm is rounded; the elbow bone must never show. The hand is an extension of the arm; it should never droop in a loose-wrist fashion or, as it is called, "break" at the wrist. The fingers are completely

relaxed, all joints loose, and are held close together but freely, the thumb held in (not open) and barely touching the middle finger. When the arm is held out to the side the audience sees the inside of the arm and part of the palm of the hand. The feeling is one of openness, lightness, yet lively expression. The arm should never be too stretched or brought too far back, giving an ugly, off-balance look.

In *arabesque*, the forward arm or arms are slightly different: stretched, with the elbow extended but not tight, and the palm down. Again, the hand is loose and extends straight from the arm; it never droops in an excessively sweet, artificial manner.

Depending on the school (Russian, French, or Italian), there are three or five basic positions of the arms. For our purposes, we will talk about the three Russian positions, for all others are variations of these three. And arm movements in a dance become so complicated that it is impossible to give a name to every position they assume anyway.

The preparation for the three positions could really be considered a fourth position, because it is a specified placement from which all other positions move and to which they all return. The arms are dropped down loosely in front of the body in a straight line from the shoulders. The hands are close together but never touching, and from shoulder to elbow no part of the arm touches the body.

For first position, the arms are brought up in front directly from the preparation on a line with the diaphragm; the same rounded arm is maintained. The arms "open side" for second position. They are held, still rounded, slightly in front of the sides of the body; they should never stick straight out from the sides like the arms of a scarecrow or ever pull back. The arms are typically held in second position for most exercises at the *barre* and for dance combinations in center floor for the first couple of years. When a correct, still, second position of the arms is achieved (and the legs are developing well), further work on the arms can begin.

Third position of the arms is the one we all assume when we imitate a ballerina: the arms circled over the head. Here again, the arms are not directly over the head but slightly forward, such that in a correct third position you can see your hands without looking up; this keeps the shoulders down and open and avoids pulling the weight backward. The hands are separated slightly, never touching.

The arms are worked on as an exercise much as the legs are exercised at the *barre*. In the lower grades the students stand still in first position and pass the arms through the various positions over and over again, working for accurate placement, fluidity, and softness. As the students move through the grades, they are given more complicated *ports de bras* that combine the movement of the arms with the correct accompanying movement of the head and changes in the position of the body. These *port de bras* exercises are axial, done from a stationary position, so it's quite another story when the student tries to use the arms in dance movement—and do more than just pass them through the classic positions.

The opportunity to practice using the arms in combination with other movements comes during *allegro* and *adagio* exercises in center floor, and eventually in advanced jumping and turning movements across the floor. The introduction of the arms into a combination is a real mark of achievement for the student, a recognition that she is making progress and is finally beginning to be able to dance. For seeming eternities ballet students are admonished to simply hold their arms out in second—and "still"—for a combination. Every beginning ballet student craves to know the arms for a movement and most will attempt to use some typical arm movements for certain steps despite the instruction to "hold the arms out to the side"—only to be embarrassed and reprimanded by the teacher for disobeying, or to find the feet becoming hopelessly tangled.

But when the arms come, when the control is slowly gained, it is as if the dancer has mastered an entire new language. Having been drilled in its vocabu-

12

12-17. A dancer's arms are as important to her technique as her legs: they help balance and propel her in certain movements, and they add expression, design, grace, and lightness to the dance. The dancer, therefore, must learn not only to place and control them for greatest advantage, but also to hold and move them softly, easily, fluidly.

Soft does not mean limp. The arms, with their elbows upheld by the inner arm muscles and their unbroken line down through the fingertips, exhibit a quiet strength. It is a strength without tension, though—as if the force and energy needed to perform movements, as dancers say, "go out through the fingers" after passing through the arm. (This page: close-ups of open and crossed arms. Facing page, 14, the arms moving from the preparatory through the first, second, and third positions, with accompanying movements of the head; 15–17, *port de bras* exercises done to develop harmonic movement of the head, arms, and upper body. Notice that the body does not lean back off its center at all, and the head does not merely drop. Rather, the spine actually bends flexibly at the waist, the head following the arm back on an even plane.)

13

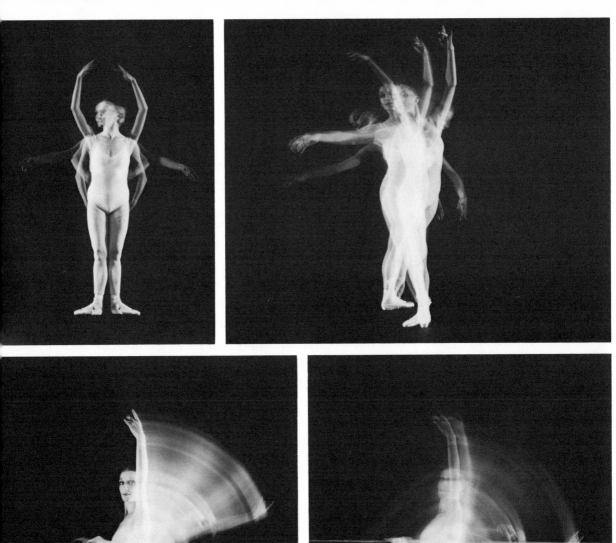

lary of prescribed positions, she can finally string them together so easily and with such variety that the individual components are lost to view. She knows how to make the *élision* or *liaison* between them so that the musicality and flow are undisturbed. She can add punctuation, inflection, tone, emotion, humor, drama.

No discussion of the arms would be complete without at least a mention of *The Dying Swan*. This lovely dramatic solo (not a part of *Swan Lake*, as many believe), created by Michel Fokine for Anna Pavlova, is a dance totally predicated on the arms. Seeing this tiny two-minute piece will do more for your understanding of the arms than all the explanation in the world. It is a moving portrayal of the last minutes of an injured swan's life as she tries painfully, tremblingly, to fly once more. It is not enough simply to say that the arms are so brilliantly and effectively done that your entire impression is "swan," not dancer. You must see it, you must feel those wings faltering and flashing up once more, and then you will know what the arms can do.

POSITIONS OF THE BODY/ÉPAULEMENT

The basic positions of the body are the ultimate evidence for the assertion that ballet is a highly specific and scientific technique, with nothing left unplanned. They are an amazing mixture of geometry and linear perspective that, without ever intruding themselves on the audience, allow almost endless diversity in the movements of the dance.

There are eleven basic positions of the body. They are defined by the angle of the body and the placement of the shoulders, arms, legs, head—and even glance—in relation to the audience (or other fixed point on the stage, for a dancer may face or move in eight different directions). Assuming the audience as the fixed point, the dancer achieves all eleven positions with the body facing directly forward (*en face*), or angled 45 degrees to its left or right. Although each position is an indispensable part of the technique, the two *effacé* ("shaded") and two *croisé* ("crossed") positions are without a doubt the most important. I'm

also going to talk a little about the two *écarté* ("separated") positions; though not quite so ubiquitous, they are, I think, the most interesting.

Effacé, leg pointed front or back, is done with the body at a 45-degree angle to the audience, with the shoulder away from the audience brought slightly forward. The term *effacé* probably was assigned because in this position the dancer's overhead arm appears to be shielding the dancer's gaze, which is directed toward the hand. While the derivation is clear, the literal translation fails to communicate the overall feeling of the position—very open, poised, and uplifted, and not "shaded" at all.

Croisé, however, is an apt name. In these positions, also done at a 45-degree angle front or back, the legs appear crossed to the audience rather than opened as in *effacé*. The head is turned out toward the audience, away from the uplifted arm, bringing the shoulder toward the audience forward. This gives a slightly more formal, haughty feeling to the position than we get in *effacé*.

All kinds of movements are done in both *effacé* and *croisé*, as you will see if you look closely. One place where you can see a *développé* in *effacé* and in *croisé*, one after the other in sharp relief, is in the opening dance of *Tchaikovsky Pas de Deux*; watch for it not only as a clear example of these positions but also as a nice, untrite use of contrast.

Écarté, unfortunately, is a position you won't see nearly as often as the others, but you will recognize it and appreciate its unique character when you do. You will usually see it as a position for a *développé*—essentially a *développé à la seconde* done diagonally to the audience. The head and upper body, perfectly square and uplifted, lean away from the raised leg over the standing leg, and the raised leg is turned out to the extreme. *Écarté* has to be absolutely flawless for it to look good—but when it is, it presents an elegant, artistic, regal design.

You may have noticed that the important positions of the body in ballet are defined, to a large extent, by the way the head is placed. This placement of the head, and its inseparable connection with the placement of the shoulders, is what

is known in ballet as *épaulement* (''shouldering''). The slightest shift in the head and shoulders can change the whole character of the position or movement; a simple shift of the gaze can entirely change the expression on the face. In *effacé*, for example, the more the head peeks out from under the arm at the audience, the more charming and saucy the dancer looks; the more thrown back the head toward the arm, the more sure, proud—even cold—the dancer looks. What this means is that there is really an infinite variety of *épaulements*, so there are almost infinite subtle variations to the basic positions of the body. Without them—or, put another way, if everything in ballet were done facing the audience straight-on—ballet would be pretty dull.

Épaulement, then, is one of those things, like the arms, that lend artistry to the dance, and make an artist of the dancer. Those dancers we see who have ''personality,'' who speak to us and elicit a responsive feeling in us, are the ones with qualities such as good *épaulement*. They are usually the great stars, the ones who can go on dancing for years after their technique has lost its edge—dancers like Fonteyn and Plisetskaya. Then there are those dancers we see who do nothing for us, whose dancing seems flat and insipid and makes us uncomfortable—sometimes nervous that they will fall and break, they are so lifeless. Frequently, they are the dancers who, with otherwise superior technique, lack good *épaulement* and, usually, nice arms.

I say ''good *épaulement*,'' for though every dancer learns the positions of the body and the basic shouldering movement, not every dancer truly absorbs them; they seem to ''sit on'' the dancer rather than come from within him. Simple as the theory of *épaulement* may seem, it is a subtle thing that dancers must begin to learn very early in the training as part of *port de bras* exercises, and then work years to acquire and incorporate as an intrinsic part of all movements. You will not be able to go to the ballet next time and say, ''Aha! There's *épaulement*,'' as you will be able to say, ''That's an *arabesque*.'' If you could, its purpose would be defeated, because it is not meant to be a separate entity. It is meant

18

18-33. The positions of the body are at the root of all poses and movements in ballet. As an element of technique they are delineated right down to the direction of the gaze, and each is rigidly and routinely learned in isolation. As an element of the dance, however, they work with magic subtlety to create shape, line, and character in movement of seemingly infinite variety, and all classroom sterility disappears.

Pictured here, and on the following pages, are nine positions of the body and, for the *effacé, croisé,* and *écarté* positions discussed in the text, examples of how these positions are incorporated into the dance. They are, left to right, *a la quatrième* (to fourth position) front; *à la seconde; à la quatrième* back . . .

21

22

efface front; *attitude* in *efface*; open *plié développé* in *efface* . . .

24–25, *effacé* back and *attitude* in that position;
26–27, *croisé* front and *attitude* in that position;
28–29, *croisé* back and *attitude* in that position . . .

écarté front and *développé* in that position . . .

and *écarté* back and *développé* in that position.

to melt into the background but at the same time embellish and add luster, like a good paste wax to a beautiful parquet floor. Gradually you will become conscious of it, most likely in connection with an individual dancer and the particular style or intuition with which he or she dances a particular role—which is as it should be.

If, however, you are impatient to learn how shouldering and the positions of the body can mean so much to the dance, I think you should pay particular attention to the dramatic *pas de deux*, the kind that has a story or a theme (such as "love") behind it. In these pieces, the dancers should be relating to each other, and the only way to really do this is through the expression of the face and the gestures of the head and upper body; the legs have never been famous communicators. Watch particularly how the woman comes under the man's arm as he turns her, as he holds her for *développés*, or as they glide across the floor together—in short, any movement where they are very close. Classic *pas de deux* are typically full of turns of various sorts, often beginning with distinct preparations and ending in distinct positions, so watch for them; the entrances and exits of the classic *pas de deux* also are frequently characterized by a sustained pose in *effacé* or *croisé*. Another time to study the positions of the body is during a series of certain traveling jumps such as *pas de chat* and *brisé*, and during many other movements that travel across the floor. Because the movement is repeated, the head and shoulders are generally held in the same position all the way across the stage. *Allegro* variations in general are a good place to observe *épaulement* and the various positions of the body, because they are typically full of fast changes of direction and little accenting movements of the head.

While on the subject of set positions of the body and how in their various forms they are incorporated into movements, it seems only natural to talk about the two classic poses in ballet as well: *arabesque* and *attitude*.

Everyone is familiar with *arabesque*. Indeed, for many people it is, along with

the third position of the arms (arms encircled overhead), the image that comes to mind at the mention of the word *ballet*: a dancer on one leg, the other extended straight behind, arms also extended.

The *arabesque* offers almost limitless possibilities for variation. It is taught, however, in specific, principal forms, which in turn vary somewhat according to method. According to Cecchetti, the famous Italian ballet master, there are five principal *arabesques*; in the French school there are two; and in the Russian, four. Generally speaking, the Cecchetti *arabesques* have become most widely accepted—although we frequently see the Russian third and fourth *arabesques*—and of these, *arabesques* in first, second, and third are most common. Detailed definitions of these three *arabesques* are of no use to anyone but the professional, but it is helpful to know the characteristics and qualities that all good *arabesques* exhibit, and to be able to recognize and appreciate their infinite variety.

An *arabesque* may be done on a flat foot, on half-toe, on *pointe*, in *demi-plié*, on one knee—in short, any way you can do it and still be on one leg. It can be done stationary, turning, promenading, or leaning forward (*penché*). It is an intrinsic part of certain other movements in ballet; for example, a *fouetté* jump in the air and a *tour jeté* (see Chapter 6) both finish in a strong *demi-plié* first *arabesque*. It can be done with the back foot pointed on the floor (as in a lunge, technically classified as an *arabesque*), raised at about a 45-degree angle off the floor, or raised to a full 90 degrees.

The leg raised to 90 degrees, or to a position parallel to the floor, is, of course, the prototype *arabesque*. The body is well centered over the standing leg, and the extended leg is turned out and perfectly straight and stretched out behind, right to the tips of the toes. In *arabesques* done in profile, the upper body is quite erect, inclining only as far forward as necessary to bring the leg up, so that there is something very close to a perpendicular angle formed where the back and the hip join. (The Russian school *arabesques* are much more inclined forward and

34-37. *Arabesque*—the emblem of classical ballet if anything is. And how appropriate, for what could be more pure, more elegant, or more appealing than its simple lines, its perfectly balanced design.

Eloquently stretched out here, exactly as an *arabesque* should be, are first, second, and third *arabesques*, respectively, and *arabesque penchée*. In the *penché*, the strong, upheld back and head are maintained, never dropped, and the body slowly inclined forward as the leg is raised higher and higher.

the back is arched.) The arms can be in virtually any position, but in the most common *arabesques* they are fully extended, one front and one back or both front, in a position roughly horizontal to the floor.

The single most important quality for an *arabesque* is that it be stretched out. The idea is to create the longest possible line from fingertips to toes: the dancer must stretch as if someone is tugging at her fingers while someone else is exerting an equal tug on her toes, and someone else is pulling equally hard at the hair on top of her head, so that she is not in the least pulled off her straight, uplifted center. Despite this maximum stretching, there is no appearance of stiffness or rigidity to the body. The arms, as usual, are soft, the hands graceful and relaxed, the squared shoulders down and the head and neck up, all serene and without tension. The body presents, as a unit, a beautiful, strong, harmonious line.

The *arabesque* I describe is the ideal one, and very difficult to achieve. It requires great strength in the back and waist area. The leg must be raised in a position and to a height that Mother Nature never intended it to, as you will appreciate if you try, holding your body erect, to raise and hold your leg up behind you as high as you can force it. It doesn't go very far, and it hurts. There is something rare about a fine *arabesque* and, I think, nothing else so stunningly elegant in ballet.

Like *arabesque*, *attitude* can be done on flat foot, *demi-pointe*, or *pointe*; on a straight leg or in *demi-plié*; turning or promenading. In the basic pose, derived from Giovanni da Bologna's statue of winged Mercury, the dancer is on one leg with the other lifted, turned out, and stretched behind with the knee bent at an angle of 90 degrees, the knee slightly higher than the foot. The arm on the side of the raised leg is overhead, with the shoulder slightly forward, and the other arm is curved at the side in second position. The back is arched and inclined forward, more than in *arabesque*.

Attitude is done facing the audience and in the *croisé* and *effacé* positions of

the body, employing *épaulement*. Many variations are possible through shifts of the arms and the direction of the head.

Consistent with the positions of the body, *attitude* is also done with the leg raised to the back or the front (there is no such thing as *arabesque* done to the front). In front *attitudes* the leg is only half bent, the foot clearly below knee level and the heel pressed forward, so that the lower leg is visible to the audience; the fully bent leg would appear cut off to the audience from the front—not very attractive.

Attitude is simpler and less dramatic than *arabesque*, but a very appealing pose nevertheless (particularly in turns, where it is shown off from every interesting perspective). The classic positions of the body give it richness and variety, while the openness and angles of the arms and legs keep it free and airy and even jaunty. It is an inspired and exciting pose.

POINTE WORK AND PARTNERING

ointe work: dancing on the toes, literally. Beautiful pink satin slippers with satin ribbons, longed for by every child ballerina until the day she is ready to put a pair on. The epitome of technique, a badge of strength. The ballet student's Last Frontier.

Contrary to what many people believe, the dancer really is up on her tiptoes when on *pointe*. People have often expressed surprise at this, assuming that the dancer is still on the flat of the toes (on half-toe) inside the shoe, with the shoe making the *pointe*—but not so. If you sit down and point your foot as much as possible, placing the toes lightly on the floor so that they don't buckle and bending the knee so that the toes are directly in line with it, it will give you an idea of what the dancer stands on—not much, is it? If your foot, like most people's, is shaped so that the toes angle back toward the little toe, perhaps only two or three toes actually touch the floor in this position. Consequently, a dancer with

a very square, or "chopped," foot has the best foot for *pointe* work, because she has a greater surface area to support her. If in addition the foot has a thick, strong ankle and a low arch—not a beautiful foot from an aesthetic point of view—it has two more advantages for *pointe* work.

Aiding the dancer is the boxed toe shoe, a lightweight, flexible satin slipper with a hardened "box" at the toe whose development around 1865 revolutionized *pointe* work (dancers had previously darned the toes of their soft slippers for support). The box has been made from balsa wood and papier-mâché; today it is made from thin plastic or two fine, stiffened layers of a canvaslike fabric with a bit of felt between. The rest of the shoe consists of a little satin with a small leather sole, the entire handmade, scientifically constructed slipper held together by nothing but a tack or two and a bit of glue. They are delicate tools, and consequently don't hold up too long under the strain of hard dancing; heat and moisture soften or "break" the box to a point where the shoes are no longer good. The lead in a big ballet can go through two or three pairs in one performance, and a ballet student typically goes through one or two pairs a month. Since shoes now cost over twenty dollars a pair, the student does everything she can to preserve them—from darning the toes to pouring a coating of acrylic floor finish into the toes to stiffen them up for just one more wearing.

But the shoes by no means do all the work—in fact, it would almost be unfair to say they do any of it. If the feet and legs are not ready—not strong enough—nothing is going to enable one to rise up onto the *pointes*. The shoe is more protection for the toes than it is real support; the boxed *pointe* is no larger than a fifty-cent piece, obviously not enough surface area to provide balance.

If a student is coming along nicely, she may don her first pair of *pointe* shoes as early as age eleven. By no means can she dance on them. At first they may be worn for about ten minutes at the end of the regular class, the student holding on to the *barre* and doing simple exercises for rising and stepping out onto *pointe*. Her first priority is to learn to go up and down smoothly and quietly

through all parts of the foot, to distribute the weight evenly over all toes, and to keep her knees straight. After a year, perhaps she will have strengthened her feet enough to be ready to take a beginning *pointe* class, a class with a *barre* and center floor work given immediately after a regular class, when the body is completely warmed up.

The first year or so on *pointe* is agony. The beginner thinks it's never going to stop hurting, that she'll never stop having blisters and throbbing toes. When the shoes come off after class, the feet have to be pushed back into shape and circulation. The student stuffs her shoes with wads of lamb's wool or wraps her toes in rabbit's fur. Strangely, as she strengthens on *pointe* (and hence as the feet begin to hurt less), it becomes evident that this overstuffing is counterproductive, and she progresses to the merest breath of lamb's wool or wraps the toes in a thin paper towel. The day arrives when the shoes don't hurt, when they are downright comfortable, and the lamb's wool serves not as padding but as a simple protection from rubbing.

There are new things to develop when a dancer advances to *pointe* work. First, of course, the muscles of the toes, the tendons of the heels, and the all-important insteps must be further strengthened and flexed, as they have not been fully developed before. The feet, and particularly the insteps, must be strong enough to become "solid" when stretched in order to support the body while on the *pointes*, and to raise and lower the body effortlessly (it is the feet that do the work in rising onto *pointe*, or *relevé*); they must be flexible enough to go from flat to *pointe* with smoothness and alacrity, as many of the most brilliant and beautiful movements on *pointe* are quick combinations of *relevés*. Now is when the meaning of that persistent term *placement* is truly understood by the dancer. To balance on *pointe*, to turn, simply to stand still, the placement must be perfect: weight over the legs, *well*-pulled-up posture and turned-out legs, tightly held buttocks and stomach, exact positions of arms and feet. The flaws in one's placement are distressingly highlighted when *pointe* work begins, and

they must be corrected. Even if one's placement is already fairly good, inadequate strength can affect it. Suddenly the arms are a problem again: *pointe* work is a new strain, and its difficulty manifests itself in an almost forgotten stiffness and unwieldiness of the arms and head. Turnout needs to be adjusted somewhat for a while; the same openness suddenly cannot be maintained on *pointe*. It is generally four or five years before one can do on *pointe* what one can do off—and ever and always movements on *pointe* are much more difficult and flaws much more apparent.

There are several things to notice when watching dancing on *pointe* that will help you understand and appreciate the technique. Like all movements in ballet, *pointe* work is done with the leg fully stretched from the hip down through the toes. The knee is tight and unyielding to the body's weight in the execution of the steps (unless the choreography calls for a bent knee—more about this later), something very difficult for a beginner to learn. However, a leg too forcibly locked curves in at the knee in an unattractive way; this hyperextension, extremely visible on *pointe*, can destroy the line.

Likewise the feet must not roll over onto the front of the toe, a problem that can be solved by greater turnout and real pulling up. The feet should be extended to the fullest and show a beautiful curve, but the point (and indeed the entire leg) is straight to the floor, not curling back and under. A curled foot throws the weight too far forward and off the tips of the toes, making the position incorrect and unappealing. Equal turnout from the hip through the feet is extremely important on *pointe* for aesthetic as well as technical reasons; as with hyperextension, even the slightest sickling of the foot in or out is extremely visible and ruins the line.

There are two basic ways to rise onto the *pointes*: One is "stepping out," or *piqué*, and the other is *relevé*. Stepping out onto *pointe* is harder than it would seem. The tendency is to bend the knee and step *up* onto it, in a movement comparable to walking upstairs; beginners do this for quite a while until they

build up the strength. The correct way is to extend the leg strongly from hip to toe, every inch stretched and the foot strongly pointed, and to step out right onto it without any break in the knee; for some movements the *piqué* is a little hop, pushing lightly off from a *demi-plié* on the other leg. The body must immediately be brought into perfect balance over the *pointe*, and the force must be just right so that the body doesn't either continue forward or fall back; the leg is absolutely perpendicular to the floor. (I can't think of anything truly analogous to *piqué*, although the action of the body is somewhat similar to that of the pole-vaulter's pole: It makes contact with the ground at an angle on a tiny point; the lower part sweeps up on a straight, strong line to a perpendicular position; and the upper part remains flexible throughout.) *Piqué* is most commonly used as a preparation for all "traveling" movements—*bourrées, piqué* and *chaîné* turns (see Chapter 7), walking—and for many *arabesques*.

There are two kinds of *relevés*, fairly interchangeable but one or the other better suited to certain steps. All dancers learn to do both equally well. One is called the "spring *relevé*," considered by some to encourage a surer centering and more precise balance. It is a little jump, beginning usually with a *demi-plié*, pushing off, and the feet imperceptibly leaving the floor at the last instant and landing on *pointe*. It is a quiet and insignificant jump, but it does serve as an impetus to arrive on *pointe*, making it the easier *relevé* for beginners. If you watch carefully you will be able to see the spring *relevé* in such movements as *pirouettes* and *sous-sus* (rising from fifth position on flats to fifth on *pointe*). Steps that involve a change in position of the feet as well as a rising on *pointe*, such as *échappé* (brisk shooting of the legs from fifth to second or fourth position), always use a spring *relevé*.

In the other *relevé*, often called "press *relevé*," the dancer simply rolls, or rises up, onto the toes. It is one continuous movement from flat feet to *pointe*, and it is done either from *demi-plié* or a straight leg, the latter, of course (without "push"), being the more difficult. This movement takes great strength. It is usu-

ally performed very slowly and deliberately, and is very beautiful to watch. You can see it most often in *relevés développés* and in *changements de pieds* on *pointe* (in which the dancer rises up and down on *pointe* in fifth position, alternately changing the foot she brings down in front each time). In the Royal Ballet's *Romeo and Juliet*, Juliet has a characteristic movement of rising up on *pointe* in the neutral position (sometimes called sixth position—feet together and straight forward, not turned out) and *bourréeing* away in that position from the others; it is almost always performed with her profile to the audience, and shows this *relevé* off slowly and beautifully.

Coming down from *pointe* properly is as important as going up. Regardless of the type of *relevé* or movement being completed, the descent must be fluid and quiet. The foot must be lowered progressively through the toes, ball of the foot, and through the heel, usually ending in *demi-plié*. Never should the foot be lowered by simply putting the heel down, or all movements, no matter how beautifully executed, would appear stiff and jerky, and the dance would seem broken up. Dancers work hard throughout their training to achieve this highly specific control over the individual muscles and tendons of the feet, to "articulate" the foot with every motion. They practice going up and coming down, going up and coming down, and raising and lowering their heels imperceptibly to change direction, because these are some of the things that will make them appear to float and glide on air.

Done well, the up-and-down movement is very pretty in itself and, repeated at fast tempos, has real flash and excitement. For this reason, in virtually every ballet that includes variations or *divertissements* for women, you will see dances that are based almost entirely on *relevé*. As a rule they are fast, lively, full of crisp, sparkling changes of the feet—and short; this type of dance on *pointe* is one of the most difficult and exhausting things in ballet.

Occasionally choreography will call for dancing on *pointe* with a bent knee. Sometimes it involves going into deep *pliés* that give the very interesting effect of

38-42. *Pointe* work, though really just an extension of the technique possessed by male and female dancers alike, is strictly a woman's domain that holds a special fascination. There is a magical, airborne, fairylike quality to even the simplest walking step on *pointe*— perhaps because all dancing on *pointe* is, in a way, a defiance of gravity. The fluidity, lightness, and speed that can be achieved on *pointe* are almost unreal, extrahuman. And then there is the downright prettiness of the highly classical work: the delicacy, the soft femininity, the quiet, woman's strength.

What a marvelous illusion it all is, for nothing could be less delicate or more down-to-earth human than the sweat and muscular strength that are behind it all. The legs work hard, of course, but the feet in particular do most of the work, not only supporting the body while on *pointe* but also providing the impetus to get there. As the photos dramatically show, the legs are fully stretched and the knees unyielding, with the "action" (and the critical strength) in the instep of the foot. Above, *piqué* onto *pointe* into *attitude*, immediately "hitting" the position, with the head over the foot; right, spring *relevé* (always from *demi-plié*) into tight *sous-sus* . . .

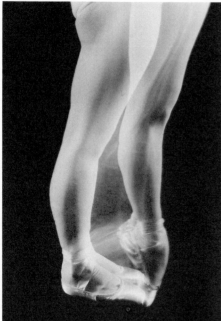

press *relevé*, left, pulled with alacrity and strength up from a flat foot; and press *relevé* again, below left, shown turned out with the heel correctly and essentially pressed forward. Below, a photo illustrating an important lesson: whether going up to or coming down from *pointe*, the foot always travels smoothly through a high half-toe on the ball of the foot.

41

looking as if the dancer is *relevé*ing from flat to *pointe* when in fact she is on *pointe* all the time (this can be seen in *Giselle*). Often, dancing with a bent knee on *pointe* involves jumping—little *changements* or tiny one-legged hops. These jumps are done in *demi-plié*, but with a difference. Instead of maintaining a straight lower leg from the knee to the floor, the leg "breaks" at the ankle, pushing the heel down slightly and the foot into what is called the hooked position. The change in position provides greater control and transfers some of the shock of landing on only two or three toes from the insteps to the more flexible knees.

Obviously, it takes tremendous force to lift the body from a position that is *already* up and from which little push can be taken, so it is remarkable that in jumps on *pointe* the lightness of the arms is yet preserved, making them look positively effortless. When a ballerina jumps on *pointe*, then, she is performing a virtuoso move, however indifferent audiences may be to its apparent ease. Its virtuosity reserves it for some of the truly special variations in classical ballet, among them Aurora's and the Bluebird variation from *The Sleeping Beauty*. In Ashton's *Romeo and Juliet*, Juliet does some remarkable *grands jetés* landing on *pointe* at the beginning of the ball scene; they are done slowly and with perfect control, holding after each.

The Sleeping Beauty in general is a veritable showcase for *pointe* technique. The Rose variation of this ballet epitomizes, to my mind, perfect mastery of *pointe*: it requires strength, grace, absolute control, perfect placement and balance, and elegance of line. It is so simple that, like Aurora's jumps, it is too often overlooked by the audience, but it is pure, unadulterated technique. As you observe work on *pointe* you will come to appreciate this variation to the degree that you will not be able to watch it without mingled feelings of suspense, thrill, and wonder; it is so fine, so agonizingly slow, so simply appealing. (See the description on pages 136–43 for more about *The Sleeping Beauty*.)

Dancing on *pointe* takes unimaginable strength and concentration, but there

is one more thing you must realize in order to appreciate it: Dancing on *pointe* is dangerous.

Every dancer has, literally, an Achilles' heel. If the Achilles tendon were severely torn, it is likely that the dancer's career would be over. A ballerina, in the constant rising up and down, is stretching and pushing that Achilles tendon beyond anything it was ever intended for.

The feet contain fifty-two bones, about a quarter of all the bones in the body. Most are small, delicately placed things, easily dislodged or fractured, and every one is open to injury from slipping or falling off the *pointe* in some way.

Why, though, should a trained dancer have to worry about falling? For one thing, the floors of most stages where ballets are performed were not designed for dancing. A ballet dancer needs a resilient, unvarnished, smooth wood floor. She almost never has it, so nearly every time she steps out she is in danger of skidding—and of falling. There are measures dancers can take to minimize their risk, but none is truly effective (see Chapter 10 for a complete discussion of how stage floors affect dancers).

Increasing the danger of falling is the speed with which many movements are done on *pointe*. Turns are faster and tighter on *pointe* than on half-toe—the fulcrum is so small—and great speed is considered to be a quality of virtuosity. But observe next time you see a dancer doing *piqué* turns very fast around the stage, whiplike *chaînés* across the floor, or consecutive *fouetté* turns: that body is *moving*. Watch how the foot is placed for each turn with no preparation, no time for consideration; it's habit, experience, long practice. One false move, one slick patch, one stray sequin, and it's all over. I cannot express the fear with which one first learns to do turns on *pointe*—even at the very slow speed at which one starts. It seems so unnatural and precarious, and the vision of a broken ankle looms enormous as you step out or spring up in a totally helpless and virtually uncontrolled manner. That vision, I think, never completely disappears, and

may be part of the reason why ballet dancers are always nervous as they wait in the wings.

When you have seen enough ballet you will be able to tell when a ballerina is holding back—because the floor is too slippery, or the shoes aren't quite right, or she just isn't feeling her absolute strongest. The best dancing is done when the dancer is fearless—and I think all ballerinas possess the fearlessness that comes with confidence and security in one's skill, tools, and experience. That fearlessness, essential to great dancing, is a certain kind of defiance—of gravity, of danger, of physical limitations—and that defiance is a kind of freedom. The freedom of great dancing, with enormous risk hovering ever present, is one of the things that make ballet perpetually exciting and new.

While we are on the subject of dancing on *pointe*—and particularly of the dangers associated with it—is a good time to say a few words about partnering, or the art of *pas de deux*. The importance of the male dancer's role in a *pas de deux* is vastly underestimated. To the inexperienced observer it appears that the *danseur* is doing nothing more than gracefully walking around. In fact, this appearance means that he is dancing his delicate and demanding part extremely well.

To understand that statement it is necessary to understand the classic *pas de deux* and what good partnering means. A *pas de deux* is a dance for two performed by a man and a woman. Its form was perfected in the great classical and Romantic ballets, in which it was used as an expression of feelings and thoughts between lovers. Every *pas de deux*, even an abstract or "modern" one, is, if not strictly romantic, an expression of a particular, intimate male-female relationship.

The objective of a good partner in the Romantic *pas de deux* is to focus the

attention of the audience on the ballerina, and make them think she is the most beautiful creature in the world. He does this by concentrating his own attention on her, never once removing his eyes from her and doing nothing, however slight, to draw attention to himself. He enhances her art by supporting her confidently and appropriately, enabling her to achieve numbers of turns or hold positions that she would not normally be able to do without his aid. He makes her look as if she floats on air, disguising the strain and difficulty of the lifts and hiding his own role in them by keeping his hands concealed behind her tutu.

All this is not easy, or as passive as it often appears. The dancer must have good technique, with particularly good feet and arms for carrying through the line made by the ballerina. He must have a fine musical sense for the many subtly graceful walking and linking movements he performs with his partner. An excellent dramatic sense is important too, so that he can express affectionate and respectful love without calling much attention to himself. The audience must get the feeling that he is wonderfully strong (and he *is*), masculine, and poised without his ever taking a position of prominence; he must possess "presence."

A ballerina relies on her partner in many ways, so his sensitivity to her particular needs and way of dancing are of paramount importance. The ideal partner knows the ballerina's musicality and phrasing, and adjusts his movements to suit hers. He is there to support her in a balance or to aid her to turn when she needs it, but is clear enough of her so as not to encumber her when she does not. If she is going to balance, he holds her in such a way that she can release his supporting hand when she is ready, not he release hers. If she is tired, or if encroaching age is robbing her strength, he carries a little more of the burden by supporting and aiding her in his sure way; in short, he compensates for her. At all times, he helps her to dance her very best, and protects her from injury as she takes the risks necessary to do so. In this sense, a ballerina's entire career can rest in her partner's hands.

The relationship between *danseur* and *ballerina*, then, is one of complete familiarity, unselfishness, and trust—as is the relationship of true lovers. And though the female is the focus of attention, both dancers must be technically and musically superb for the *pas de deux* to work. The nature of the relationship and the requirements for the dancers have produced and will continue to produce some great and interesting partnerships. They enable us to see two exceptional dancers alone together, showing us the best of their art. And they give us the pleasure of watching a fine partnership evolve, change, and mature over the years.

Movement

True movement in ballet implies a change in position from one point to another. This in turn implies some sort of direction—up, around, across—and that the whole body must be involved. In ballet, there are three groups of such movements: jumps and beats, turns, and linking movements. Within each group, each movement combines all the elements of placement and as such is a complete entity, an end in itself, a movement for movement's sake.

JUMPS AND BEATS

*J*umps and beats are the hallmark of *allegro*, or fast, lively dancing. As contributors to the well-rounded, perfectly complete technique of classical ballet, they give ballet not only excitement and brilliance, but also something without which ballet can scarcely be imagined: a vertical dimension.

It has been over three hundred years since the ballet audience, used to *terre à terre* (along the ground) dancing in a horizontal plane, first witnessed a dancer jump up off the floor into the air. Yet today's audiences are far from jaded; they are still thrilled and impressed by jumps and their embellishing sister, beats.

A dancer must possess two qualities to jump: elevation and *ballon*. Elevation is, logically, the dancer's ability to attain height in a jump, as measured from the ground to the tips of the dancer's pointed toes in the air. *Ballon* is elasticity, or bounce, such that the dancer bounds up lightly from the floor, suspends for a moment in midair, and lands softly and smoothly, ready to bounce up again like

a rubber ball. The two qualities go hand in hand—one is not much good without the other—and all great jumpers have them.

In saying "have them," or "must possess" them, I don't mean that a dancer is born with them. He may be fortunate enough to have been born with, for example, a very pliant Achilles tendon, and this will certainly give him some advantage, but for the most part elevation and *ballon* must be developed—like everything else in ballet. And like everything else in ballet, they are developed through hard work and the tedious repetition of exercises, first at the *barre* and then in the center.

The development of correct posture; a strong back; good turnout and positions of the feet; and a deep, flexible *demi-plié* in which the heels are kept firmly on the floor are essential before any serious study of *allegro* can begin. Students must acquire a strong *frappé*, a movement in which the foot, beginning with a small beat *sur le cou-de-pied*, is extended out strongly (action from the knee), striking the floor with the ball before fully extending; during the final extension, the dancer rises onto half-toe or *pointe* on the standing leg. The striking or brushing movement, coupled with the extension and push up on the standing leg, is the basis of the *jeté* in its many forms.*

Students also must practice rising up on half-toe from *demi-plié* and then lowering the feet again into *demi-plié*, all in one smooth, continuous movement. The feet are raised and lowered in a fluid progression from the heel to the ball of the foot and then from the ball of the foot to the heel, as if they are a piece of tape being pulled up from a table and then smoothed back down; the back is held erect.

Students learn the fundamentals of *allegro* at the *barre*, facing it and holding

Frappé is executed as a dance step as well as an exercise, usually on *pointe* and double-beaten (in front of and behind the ankle before extending).

on with both hands for support. They start off doing little jumps in first, second, and fifth positions, paying special attention to stretching the legs and feet strongly while in the air, keeping the back straight and the shoulders down (at the beginning of the study of jumps, there is a chronic disappearance of necks into hunched shoulders), and landing in *demi-plié* with the heels on the floor.

These same little jumps are done in the center. Without the *barre* for support, the strain in the arms, neck, and shoulders is a greater problem, and a weak back leads to a jerking movement of the upper body during the jumps. The students work to keep the upper body relaxed, to hold the arms loosely and still, to hold the back firmly—and, it is hoped, to attain some height.

The mastery of these little jumps, along with mastery of *assemblé*, form the foundation for all other jumps and for beats. *Assemblé* is a jump from fifth position *demi-plié* to fifth position *demi-plié* (opposite foot front) in which the dancer brushes one foot along the floor and extends the leg out to the side (in second position) to a height of 45 or 90 degrees, simultaneously straightening and pointing the other leg. It is actually a very difficult jump, but must be introduced early in the training in an elementary form to facilitate the learning of other jumps because the *plié*, brush, stretch, *plié* sequence is fundamental to *allegro*. *Assemblé* itself can be very grand when done to 90 degrees. Particularly exciting are *assemblé* turning, or beaten and *volé* ("flying," "traveling"), combined with complementary movements of the arms.

It would be nice if we in the audience could identify every jump in ballet by name; it would be personally satisfying, and a lot easier than saying "those jumps in which the dancer does a sort of suspended split in the air, pushing off from one leg and landing softly on another" (*grands jetés*). Learning the name of every jump is impossible, however, for anyone but a dancer. First of all, there are so many jumps: jumps from both feet to both feet, in or into various positions; jumps from one foot to another; jumps that combine other elements, such

as turns; jumps from both feet to one foot, or from one foot to both feet; consecutive jumps on one foot. Big jumps, little jumps, beats. Their diversity is wondrous.

Furthermore, many jumps are just too complicated to explain in words; their descriptions would be longer than the last paragraph, and impossible for the lay person to follow. Even if you had seen a particular jump many times, you would probably never recognize it in a description.

Finally, many steps go by a few different names—a result of their having been taught in so many different national schools and by so many master teachers. It gets confusing. Besides, most names of jumps are too long to be anything but awkward in conversation: *grand jeté dessus en tournant battu* and *assemblé soutenu en tournant en dehors* do not exactly roll off the tongue.

Fortunately, beyond being able to identify in elementary form some of the jumps seen most often in ballet (and you will be able to after studying the photos and descriptions provided), knowing the names of jumps is of little value to the balletgoer. It is much more useful to learn about their execution, and to cultivate an appreciation for their richness and variety.

It is also much easier. Simply go to the ballet as often as you can and watch with attention. Notice the various components of the jump, from preparation to landing. See if you can recognize some of the basic ballet positions or poses in the jump. You may discover that a single jump involves not only a jump, but also a turn in the air, a midair beat with the legs, a change of feet from push-off to landing, and a finishing pose in *arabesque*. Or you may notice that the dancer's legs are in *attitude* while in the air, one front and the other back. Or that some of the most awe-inspiring jumps are those done barely off the floor.

With experience will naturally come an interest in execution, and you will find yourself concentrating on the feet and arms from time to time. It is then that you will be struck by a simple but momentous fact: *Every jump begins and ends with demi-plié.* Stated another way, this axiom says: There can be no jumps

without *demi-plié*. The *demi-plié* provides the spring to get the dancer up in the air, the soft landing, and the ability to rebound into the air for another jump. (You can see this yourself by standing with your feet together and trying to jump up and down in place: you have to bend your knees to get up. And if you don't bend your knees coming down, your landing is jolting and stiff, and you can't get back up again—to say nothing of the shinsplints you'll develop.) Each time the dancer lands, the heels must come down firmly onto the floor; the *demi-plié* should never be done on the balls of the feet. This is tough, sometimes impossible, in a series of jumps at a fast tempo—try jumping in place again, very fast, and forcing your heels to "hold" the floor for a second each time you land—but it is the rational ideal the dancer works for. For the dancer, it means mastery of technique; for the audience, it means clean, sharp jumps that are beautiful to watch.

If you did your experimental jumping in front of a full-length mirror, you probably noticed that the force of jumping had a not-terribly-attractive effect on some parts of your body. Most likely, your upper body jerked back and forth as you jumped, your head and neck became painfully strained, and your arms stiffened out to your sides. That the dancer jumps with his body erect, still, and relaxed, his arms moving freely and independently of the body and legs or held gracefully and graciously open, is remarkable, and shows the all-important muscle control at work. The muscles of the thighs, buttocks, stomach, and (particularly) back absorb and hide all the tension so that the dancer goes up with an air that says, "See how easy it is? I fly like a bird." When compared to the way the gymnast runs across the floor, strain showing in every muscle, to do a simple *grand jeté*, the sudden, easy jump of the ballet dancer seems a stunning achievement.

The "sudden" quality of the big, high jump is another little deception of the dancer worth knowing about. The dancer does, like the gymnast, build up some impetus for the jump, but in a way so smooth as to be almost imperceptible. His

43-47. The lyric "flies through the air with the greatest of ease" aptly applies to a dancer performing any of ballet's great jumps: the dancer bounds up, soaring high and moving through or holding difficult positions, making it look relaxed and effortless. Nothing in ballet is more commanding than that moment at the pinnacle of the big jump, when each member of the audience is held transfixed by a person like himself, but then again—not like himself. In that instant, the audience receives an impression of dynamism, strength, defiance, and a control that is almost lordly—mixed with a touch of devil-may-care or even aloof reserve.

The jumps of ballet may be too numerous and complex to describe, but they all have certain common characteristics that combine to give us this impression. Most fundamentally, of course, are height, or elevation, and bounce and loftiness, or *ballon*, which helps give jumps their qualities of smoothness and surprise. An erect back and impeccably stretched legs speak strength, energy, and control, and soft, independent arms flaunt confidence and ease.

But it is the position, or design, of the body in the air that is the great thing, the thing that elicits the wonder, and takes the breath away. This page: *grand jeté*. Opposite page, top: two views of a *saut de chat* (like a *grand jeté*, except that the front leg, instead of brushing straight up, passes through *attitude*). Opposite page, bottom: *sissone* to the side; *saut de basque*.

48

49

48-51. The elegant *tour jeté* combines a fast turn in the air and whiplike change of the legs with a high jump. The action is so quick that seeing the peak of the jump is difficult even with a camera. Here (48–50) the jump was captured in the air at three different points after the turn; the photos show the right leg, which was brushed up as the dancer pushed off the ground from the left leg, coming down for the landing, and the left leg going up behind for the finishing pose in *arabesque*. The movement photograph (right) shows the preparatory steps that give impetus for the jump, the second just before the right leg brushes up and the dancer "takes off," and the landing—so that the three shots above all occur in that faint blur visible above the landing pose.

52-55. Another wonderfully quick, complicated, and hard-to-capture jump is the *pas de chat* (''step of the cat''). It is nearly impossible for the camera to catch the jump quite at its peak and therefore do justice to the dancer's *pas de chat*, but these shots are useful for showing a sequence that cannot be easily visualized from a description: the body traveling in an arc, from fifth position pushing off from the back right leg, bringing it up to meet the left (more closely than shown here), and the left leg lowering first to close in fifth behind. Quick as a cat—but sometimes seen ''slow motion'' in a lift during a *pas de deux* .

56

57

58

59

56-60. The steps of the *petite* and *grande batterie* are perhaps the finest vehicles for exhibiting that marvelous hovering quality, *ballon*, and for presenting some of the prettiest lines in all ballet. But it is only with fully stretched legs and feet, thighs together, and calves (not ankles) making the beat that the exquisite perfection of line shown in this group of photographs is possible. From top left: *cabriole* back (56), *cabriole* front (57) and its lovely landing (58); *brisé* (59) and *entrechat* (60).

60

method is a series of little running and gliding steps, many of them technically small jumps themselves, that precede the final preparatory *demi-plié* (these steps are discussed in Chapter 8). When the dancer at last springs up into the air, we wonder how he got there. The juxtaposition of the big jump and the low, little steps is one of the things that makes the jump exciting and appear even higher than it is.

Another thing that can make a jump exciting is a beat—the striking of both legs together or of one leg against the other. As an embellishment of a jump, the beat is usually done after the primary movement of the jump and just before the landing; that is, it is sort of sneaked in as a little bonus. The effect is to add a bit of flash or brilliance to the jump, another degree of complexity, a touch of daring virtuosity. Getting those beats into a jump that is already so complicated that there is barely time in the music to do it well is difficult indeed, and exciting to see. The entire jump must be that much faster and cleaner, and done with that much more boldness and strength. Consequently, beats are very tiring, and we can only marvel at a dancer who can do them repeatedly without getting droopy and sloppy.

Almost any jump can be embellished with a beat; the name of the jump then has the descriptor *battu* ("beaten") tacked onto the end (e.g., *assemblé battu*). In addition, some jumping steps in ballet are by their very nature beaten; that is, they wouldn't exist without the beat. The most famous of these is the *entrechat*. The word *entrechat* means "interwoven, braided," and that is exactly the condition the legs simulate in the step. The dancer jumps from fifth position straight up, slightly opens the legs and changes them front to back, beats the legs, then opens and changes them again, so that he lands with the same foot in front as when he began. This is called *entrechat quatre* ("four"), for the total number of position changes made by both legs (two for each leg).

The *entrechat quatre*, along with other jumps such as *brisé* (one foot brushing out from behind the other, beating in front, and returning) and *royale* (jump,

straight up, beat without changing feet, then change for landing), is part of what is known as the *petite batterie* (small beating steps). They are the more elementary beats, executed low to the ground. There is also a *grande batterie* (large beating steps), which requires a higher spring off the floor. It comprises *entrechat six* and up, all "big" jumps that are embellished with a beat, and another beat you have probably seen many times, the *cabriole*. In *cabriole* done to the front, the dancer swings the back leg forward and up to an angle of 90 degrees, immediately jumping off from the other leg and bringing it up to meet the leg already in the air; the legs beat together with a force and elasticity that pushes the first leg a little higher, and the dancer lands again on the leg he jumped from. *Cabriole* is often seen done in sequence front, back, front, back, a combination that always reminds me of a hummingbird hovering over a flower.

Every audience, regardless of sophistication, loves big jumps and beats because they are thrilling and spectacular. In being caught up by the spectacle, however, the audience sometimes overlooks subtler but more demanding and better-executed steps, and is too frequently taken in by flashy but bad dancing. Be sure to look at the little jumps as well as the big, for it is these that, at fast tempo, are the most difficult of all. The changes of feet, beats, *relevés*, and changes of direction that characterize combinations of little jumps must be done quickly, sharply, energetically, and without hesitation. It is exhausting work. And remember, it is one thing to do multiple beats while soaring high in the air or being held aloft by a partner, but quite another to do them, and do them well, in jumps where the feet are barely off the ground—and then only for a split second.

I keep emphasizing that jumps and beats must be "clean" and "sharp." Like turns, jumps are useless, no matter how high they go, if they are not executed with tightly held positions and neat landings. In beats, it is the *legs* that beat, not the feet. The calves must strike together sharply so there is a little rebound, like the motion of your leg when your knee is tested for reflexes. The thighs should

be touching and the entire leg turned out from the hips; in beats done *en face,* you should be able to see both heels from the audience. Both legs, from the thighs to the tips of the toes, should be stretched to the limit. A limp leg or droopy foot in a beaten step makes it look like mush. Actually, the strongly extended and turned-out leg is not a requirement for beats only; it is essential for any jump.

Although women can and do execute the steps of the *grande batterie,* they are mainly the province of the male dancer, whose natural strength and boldness suit him for such movements. They can always be seen in the man's variations of Classical *pas de deux*—pieces particularly designed to show off, among other things, the man's jumping prowess. The big jumps and beats also form the basis for some short ballets that were choreographed for a dancer with virtuoso ability in *allegro. Tarantella,* choreographed by George Balanchine for Edward Villella, is one such work, and affords a great opportunity for studying jumps and beats.

Unfortunately, a paucity of good male dancers in the 1960s and early '70s accustomed the balletgoing public to seeing, and accepting as normal, a lot of sluggishness, sloppy footwork, and stiff bodies—so virtuoso parts are not always danced with virtuoso ability. As attitudes toward ballet change, however, and more men enter ballet professionally, the number of good male dancers increases. Coupled with the increasing discrimination of audiences, the men's technique should, within a decade, be on a par with the women's. In the meantime, we can learn to distinguish and applaud what *is* good in what we see, and to appreciate some of the less spectacular though perhaps more truly amazing aspects of *allegro.*

TURNS

By now it is obvious that ballet dancing would be very flat and dull indeed without the endless variety of the movement of the arms, the finishing touch lent by *épaulement*, or the vertical dimension supplied by jumps. The more we learn about the various components of the dance, the more we realize how truly unified the classical technique is, with each component adding a special quality to the dance as a whole and enhancing the others. It becomes impossible to imagine the dance without one of its elements.

Consider turns, for example. What *would* ballet dancing be without them? How would the female dancer, for whom turns are a specialty, show off her mastery of technique? What possible substitute for turns could be found to provide a breathtaking finish to an exciting variation? Probably the most famous moment in ballet is in *Swan Lake*, act 3, when the Black Swan, walking onstage

and taking a firm preparation, goes into her thirty-two *fouetté* turns. Would the Black Swan be the same Black Swan to us without them?

No, certainly not, because turns—like the arms, the shouldering, the jumps—have qualities all their own. An obvious one, which characterizes most turns, is speed—a speed that defies its danger with the confidence that comes with perfect balance and control; a speed more brilliant than that with which, say, beats are done, because it involves the entire body, and often propels the dancer across the stage at an awesome rate.

A subtler quality is what I can only call, rather inadequately, a kind of exoticism or rarefaction. Turns have a rather spiritual, ephemeral quality, certainly—particularly when done slowly and distantly under the arm of a lover in a romantic *pas de deux*—but it is a little more than that. There is something about turns that is out of the realm of normal experience. They are the one thing in ballet with which we cannot identify at all, but can only look at with appreciation and a little wonder. As do dancers, we run, walk, skip, hop, jump and leap, stand on our toes—but spinning in circles on one leg, we don't even approximate.

Perhaps this is why turns take longer to master than any other movement in ballet. Dancers never stop practicing them, spending spare moments in rehearsal or between classes turning in front of the mirror. Turns are not—like a good *arabesque*, nice arms, or complete turnout—principally developed through a series of exercises. They are, instead, arrived at by constant practice and repetition of the whole movement; they "come" to the dancer. This may sound a little esoteric at first, but it's the simplest truth. Turns are mostly a matter of feel.

That is not to say that there is no technique to turns, no correct or even essential way to do them so they come off: The execution of all turns has certain requirements. To begin with, there must be a strong preparation, the dancer relying, as ever, on the indispensable deep *demi-plié* and correct position of the feet. The body—as ever—must be pulled up and squared and centered over the

61. This picture shows the very essence of successful turns—the all-important preparation and spring up onto the leg. The dancer is centered over the legs, which are in a good, turned-out fourth position *demi-plié*. The spring is straight up, the body remaining in perfect alignment; the open (side) arm is brought gently but purposefully in front. This position reached, the rest—the turn itself—is relatively easy.

legs. Were it not—for example, if the hips were turned, a shoulder pulled back, or a fourth position too open—the body would be off balance on rising for the turn and would invariably tip over.

After the preparation comes what is probably the most critical part of the turn, even though the actual turning has not yet begun: the act of springing up (or stepping out, depending on the type of turn) onto the toes of one leg. The dancer, having taken her preparation with the feet firmly holding the floor, pushes off from both feet equally, and rises high on the toes of the forward leg, bringing the other leg into the position it will maintain during the turn. The body thus comes directly over the foot and is inclined just slightly forward. Inclined, not bent; there is no break at the waist or neck or anywhere else. The body is still absolutely erect.

It is difficult to communicate how really important such a simple-sounding thing is. But as you see turns done time after time you will notice when they are not quite right, and it will almost always be because something went wrong in getting up on the leg. You will notice that some dancers (particularly among the men) "sit" in their turns, giving a sluggish, earthbound impression. Probably they are on a low rather than a high half-toe, and bent forward a little at the waist; in short, they are not pulled way up over the leg. Similarly, you might occasionally see a ballerina, while doing multiple turns with a partner, begin to lean, and the man gently support her; she was "off her leg" (not centered over her foot) when she began. As I have heard teachers say many a time, "Just get up there properly over the foot, and you will turn automatically; you don't need to do anything else."

And so the body does, automatically, begin to turn. To prevent dizziness, ensure complete revolutions that land precisely where they began, and keep the dancer on course in a series of traveling turns, the dancer uses a technique called *spotting*. This means, quite simply, that she keeps her eyes focused for as long as possible on a spot before her as she turns, bringing her head around quickly at the last moment and again fixing her eyes steadily on the spot. Spotting is critical to the success of whiplike, multiple turns, and the dancer must "feel the front" every time she comes around to face the audience.

Other than spotting and making the correct preparation and spring up onto the leg, the dancer need do nothing more than keep the lifted leg well turned out to help bring her around, and bring the arm, opened to the side during preparation, gently in to meet the other in first position. Some energy in this movement helps the turn, but any real force (i.e., swinging the arm in) will topple the dancer off her leg rather than help propel her around.

After one complete revolution—or two, or four, or six—comes the landing. The landing is as much a part of the turn as the preparation or the actual moment of turning is; the turn is simply not complete without it. And if the landing is not done properly, the turn, no matter how many flashy revolutions it has entailed, has been a failure.

To land, the dancer must come straight down from the turn into (depending on the type of turn) a solid position *demi-plié* (usually fourth or fifth); the body should remain erect, the head up and the eyes front. A solid position in *demi-plié* is one in which the toes and heels are firmly and evenly pressed to the floor, the knees are open and deeply bent, and the body is pulled up and held still. If anything in ballet sounds relatively easy, this does—and it is a fact that, theoretically, the finish of a turn is an elementary matter. But remember that most turns are characterized by speed; the dancer is whipping around at a fair clip when she is required to lower her body suddenly in an exact spot with her feet in a precise position—to stop dead without a waver of the body. Well, it's not possible to stop short in your car without being jolted a little, and it's similar here.

Unavoidably, the difficulty of landing—and of turning in general—occasionally shows, usually in a bouncing, and sometimes even a kind of hopping, movement of the feet. It is so hard to keep those heels from coming up off the floor,

but they must stay there—in *demi-plié* and as the legs straighten. Coming down in position is also much easier said than done. Because of the momentum, and particularly if the balance has been precarious and the body is not perfectly erect, the legs tend to end up too far apart, or too open or crossed. Even though the feet have hit the ground, the body will rock a little in a struggle for equilibrium, and possibly topple off the spot. Knowing that the word *finish* in reference to a turn can have a double meaning, however, dancers exert themselves tremendously to land from even the most disastrous turns with a show of security and confidence; the audience, as a result, almost never realizes there has been a problem.

These are the basic principles of turns. Different preparations, and different positions of the legs and arms, produce a treasury of turns that, like jumps, are almost endless in their variety. There are turns on two legs, and turns on one leg that, theoretically, could be done from any of the five positions. There are turns in *attitude* and *arabesque*. There are stationary turns, and turns that travel in a straight line or in a circle. There are turns done to the inside (*en dedans*), or toward the supporting leg, and to the outside (*en dehors*), or away from the supporting leg. Of them all, most prevalent are probably *pirouette*,* *tour à la seconde* (turn in second position), *fouetté* turns (*fouetté rond de jambe en tournant*, "whipped circular movement of the leg while turning"), *piqué* turns, and *chaîné* turns (*tours chaînés déboulés*, "linked turns rolling like a ball").

The *pirouette* is certainly the most familiar turn in ballet. It is the corkscrew-like turn on one leg in which the foot of the other leg is pointed in to touch the standing leg in a variable position between the knee and the ankle (usually a sort of low *passé*), forming a triangular space between the legs. It is most frequently started from fourth or fifth position, and is almost always done at the very least

---

*Strictly speaking, there are many types of *pirouettes*. For simplicity here, the word *pirouette* always means the basic *pirouette sur le cou-de-pied*. The word *tour*, or simply turn, is used instead of the word *pirouette* for the other types discussed.

as a double—two revolutions before coming down. *Pirouettes* are also done in a series: that is, the dancer lands in position and pushes off again between turns. Often these series involve a change of direction (from inside to outside, for example) or a change of leg. Though also done solo, *pirouettes* are the only turns done supported by a partner. The *pas de deux*, therefore, is a surefire place to see them in all their infinite variety; there probably isn't a *pas de deux* in existence that doesn't contain *pirouettes*.

The *pirouette* is an especially important turn because it is a kind of building block for the more difficult *fouetté* turns or *tour à la seconde*. Consequently, a dancer learns *pirouette* very early in the training and works on it for years before the other turns are introduced. The student first gets the feeling of turning the body during exercises at the *barre*, first on two feet and then on one, first a half-turn and then a full turn. She begins practicing turns in the center (unsupported) with only the preparation, the spring up, and the landing. Only when she can pull up well over the leg and land in proper position is the element of turning—as if an afterthought—added. Beginning with quarter-turns, she progresses to half-turns, and finally goes all the way around. In this way the student gradually develops the "feel" I was talking about before: where the balance is, how much force with which to move the arm, and so on. Over the rest of a dancer's career she continues to practice full turns. They are a long time coming. As one teacher said to a moaning and groaning class of students struggling over *pirouettes*—first in fourth, then in fifth, then in second position—"Oh, don't worry; after about a million of them you'll get it."

Tour à la seconde is just like a *pirouette* except that the leg is lifted from second position on the floor straight up into a very turned-out second position at 90 degrees and held there for the turn; the leg is kept well turned out and seems to lead the body around. (This turn to the inside is started and finished in fourth, with the leg brought into second for the turn; it is not seen often.) *Tour à la seconde* requires great strength in the thighs and buttocks; it was, for a long

time, the exclusive domain of the male dancer. Although many women do them well nowadays, they are still principally a male step. Solo variations by men frequently include them done in series as single turns lowering on the standing leg to *demi-plié* between each, and occasionally as doubles (without lowering) by a very strong and accomplished dancer. It is a stunning, virtuoso turn.

Fouetté turns are the female counterpart of *tour à la seconde*, the female dancer's virtuoso turn; I cannot recall ever having seen this turn done by a man in a performance. *Fouetté* turns are a series of single turns in which the leg in the air whips around in a quarter-circle as the body turns, touching just behind and in front of the knee before being thrust out in *croisé* front as the dancer sinks into a brief *demi-plié*, facing the audience, before beginning another revolution. It is as complicated as it sounds, with a lot to do and a very little time to do it in. Bringing the foot well in to the knee instead of letting it dangle outside is no small accomplishment, and the movement of the raised leg (this is the only turn in which the raised leg is not kept still) of course makes it much more difficult to maintain the balance. And the constant up, down, up, down of the dancer on the *pointe* of one foot, each time taking a sure feel of the front, requires not only great strength in the legs and feet but also very secure placement.

Female dancers are so good these days that all leading ballerinas and many regular dancers can do the once rare thirty-two *fouetté* turns of the famous Black Swan *pas de deux* in *Swan Lake*. Nevertheless, it is still a virtuoso move and always exciting to see someone who can not only do them but do them exceptionally well, always coming down exactly front, without the least gravitation from the spot, and with an unflagging leg.

In contrast to the difficulty of *fouetté* turns is the relative simplicity of *piqué* turns. Though simple, they are worth mentioning because they are a very common turn in women's variations and are extremely pretty when done well.

Piqué ("pricked") means to step out sharply right onto the *pointe* of one leg, keeping the leg perfectly straight, and simultaneously centering the body over it.

There is no *relevé* up onto the toes, but rather, when the dancer is in *pointe* shoes, a kind of daring little hop. As the dancer steps out, the other leg is brought up and pointed just in front or in back (depending on the direction of the turn) of the leg in a position similar to that of *pirouette*. The dancer turns, puts the other leg down in *demi-plié*, and then "hops" out again for another turn. In this way the dancer travels forward across the stage, either on a diagonal or in a circle. *Piqué* turns are always done in series, with the arms gently opening and closing as the dancer turns. Double or even triple revolutions before touching down in *demi-plié* are sometimes alternated with single turns for a dazzling effect. In the last act of *La Bayadère*, for example, Nikiya moves across the stage, her lover Solor behind her, in a repeating pattern of two single *en dehors piqué* turns (called "lame-duck turns") and a double *piqué* turn finishing in *arabesque*. It is lovely.

It is *chaîné* turns, though, that in many ways are the truest and most exciting display of the dancer's turning prowess. In *chaîné* turns, the dancer spins, as if propelled by the velocity of her turns, in tiny, tight circles across the stage. While the movement of *pirouettes* and *fouetté* turns can be likened to the pumping and spinning of a top, that of *chaînés* cannot because they neither have the up-down movement nor stay on one spot. It is more like the movement of a tornado, or twister, across a plain; it whirls with an internal speed, and rushes forward with another. When *chaînés* are done in a circle (imagine the difficulty of turning circles within a circle, when the dancer's "spot," or front, changes slightly with every revolution), the movement is exactly like the rotation of the spinning earth around the sun.

It would be difficult to recognize *chaîné* turns from a technical description alone without such images in mind; the turns are done too quickly and with almost imperceptible movement. Furthermore, a definition sounds deceptively simple; to wit: *Chaînés* are half-turns done on alternating legs in a continuous series. As preparation for *chaîné* turns, the dancer *demi-pliés* on one leg and

steps out sharply onto the toes of the other leg. After a half-turn, she puts her other foot down close in front of the foot she just turned on, does a half-turn on the new foot, and so on. Throughout the series of turns, both legs are perfectly straight and the feet well pointed; the foot not making the turn is just barely off the floor. The heels are very close together and the legs are turned out, so that the dancer is in what is really a first position on *pointe*. Once the turns get going, the tiny steps of the feet and the whipping of the head are the *only* movements of the body.

Compared with doing multiple full turns on one leg while holding the other in a prescribed position, half-turns with both feet practically on the ground may sound awfully easy; the movement of the feet even sounds a little like walking. But there are a few things about *chaînés* that make them a true virtuoso move. One of them is speed. *Chaînés* are done at a very fast tempo—each half-turn in half- or even quarter-beats of the music. The speed, plus the added dimension of forward movement, make *chaînés* the most dizzying of turns.

Only perfect placement and control allow a dancer to do sixteen and even thirty-two counts of *chaîné* at breakneck speed. Because there is virtually no movement of the body once the turns begin (at fast tempos, there isn't even time to open and close the arms slightly to assist the turning), the dancer must step out over the leg with the back erect and somewhat forward, and hold it strongly throughout the turns. Likewise the legs and buttocks and the stomach muscles must be held tight and not let go even for a second, or the turns will fall apart. At the end of the series of turns—frequently building in a crescendo of speed for a breathtaking finish to a variation—the dancer must use her perfect control to come to a sudden, dead halt in a graceful pose, as if she's just been standing there all along. That is the great thing about *chaîné* turns. When they are beautifully done, we can't *see* the dancer do them. She just moves, magically. And that is what ballet is all about.

Preparation, placement, getting up high over the leg, spotting, landing in position—these are what turns are all about, and where the ''feel'' comes in. ''Think of balance,'' the teachers say, ''and pulling up. You must come down in tight fifth, good *demi-plié* or . . . [they shrug] nothing. The head snaps your turns; . . . six turns is in your head.''

 LINKING MOVEMENTS

Dancing is a kind of language, and a ballet is, in a way, a story or idea worked out in dance sentences. The breathtaking lifts, brilliant jumps and turns, and astonishing sustained poses are like adjectives and adverbs; they are embellishments with an uncanny power to impress upon the mind, though they constitute only a small part of the dance sentence. The linking or auxiliary movements that connect them together—like subjects, conjunctions, auxiliary verbs, articles, and pronouns—tend to go unnoticed, though they are the real structural underpinnings of ballet.

This is not necessarily bad. In fact, if you told a choreographer or dancer that you didn't really notice the linking movements between all the big jumps and turns, chances are he would say, "Good. Then I have used them [performed them] well." It would be a tribute to his art.

Although linking movements are not meant to make a big impression on the audience, they are nevertheless extremely important in the dance—in many ways, *are* the dance. As such, they can be the greatest creative resource of a choreographer, and can reveal some interesting things about individual dancers and dancing.

It would seem, then, that there is a little more to linking movements than the mere connecting of steps. True. Linking movements have important mechanical functions in ballet. They allow the dancer to transfer his weight from one leg to the other; to change direction in a single, swift movement, and, simply, to get from one step to another. Frequently the dancer does not even move from the spot, and the linking movement is imperceptible. In a simple *coupé* ("cut"), for example, the dancer puts one foot down to replace the other on the spot so the other may step or brush out for the next movement. A split-second movement in place, and yet *coupé* is crucial to ballet, particularly in combinations of small jumps and beats.

Linking movements also provide the majority of the horizontal movement in a ballet; without them, a dancer would remain virtually on one spot. They include walking, gliding, running, and waltzing steps that enable the dancer to move forward, backward, sideways, on a diagonal, or in a circle. Many of these steps are not much different from what most people define as walking, running, or waltzing. The arms will be placed differently, the legs turned out or extended, or the dancer on *pointe*, but the basic step will be the same. Others—like *glissade, pas de bourrée,* and *pas de basque*—are unique to ballet, designed to achieve a change of feet, movement across a distance, and a pretty pattern on the floor all in one. Nearly all linking movements can be done diminutively to move a few inches, or expansively to move completely across the stage; the speed and size of the movement can alter its character to the extent that it is scarcely recognizable as the same one. Probably the most familiar of this kind of movement is *bourrée* on *pointe*. Done "small," it is a dainty stamping or pricking movement of the feet for moving slowly across space. Done "large," it is a

stronger, sweeping movement for propelling the dancer rapidly across the stage.

In providing the horizontal dimension in ballet, linking movements also make possible the vertical dimension because they give the dancer impetus for the big jumps and *grande batterie*. At the same time, they set off the big movements by way of contrast: they are understated rather than bold, smooth rather than sharp. They make all the movements that surround them appear bigger, more brilliant, and more exciting.

Smoothness of execution is essential if linking movements are not to detract from the more climactic moves. Though the movement of the feet in the various linking movements is not the least bit complicated, the steps are, nevertheless, extremely difficult to do well. They must be done with subtle grace and lightness, but with exact placement of the feet so that the dancer doesn't look (as is often the case) as if he is simply running. Because the feet move virtually beat-for-beat with the music, linking movements require a greater musicality and sense of timing than perhaps any other movements in ballet; indeed, they are the true "dancing" movements, many of them having been perfected under high standards of grace, precision, nobility, and finesse as parts of social dances in the royal courts centuries ago. They are the thing that makes ballet a continuous flow of movement rather than a mere series of designated steps, and are, therefore, the truest test of the danceability of a dancer—that is, his natural but developed gift for moving to music with perfect grace, tempo, and artistic judgment, as if he has become part of the music, and the music moves him, free and unresisting.

The use of linking movements also says something to us about a choreographer's understanding of music and the essence of ballet. Some contemporary choreographers, in an effort to be modern and to appeal to the audience on a grand scale, neglect the use of linking movements in favor of more glamorous and spectacular moves. The result, more often than not, is a ballet whose awkward abruptness is offensive or unappealing to the senses, or that is more an acrobatic display than a ballet; such ballets are built on a total disregard for the music. It takes an extremely creative, skillful, and musical choreographer to make a ballet that is almost devoid of linking movements yet has a flowing, musical quality and technical and visual beauty. Mr. Balanchine can do it. But even Mr. Balanchine would not attempt to make a ballet from a lively waltz or mazurka without including linking movements, because such music cries out for a continuous flow of danceable movements—for gliding *glissades* and bouncy *balancés*.

Linking movements can form the basis of a dance, or can merely be necessary mechanical supplements to other steps. But in every case they are indispensable to creating smoothness, feeling, and shape in a ballet.

Dance

After about ten years of working hard to master the correct placement and execution of steps, the ballet student is ready to enter a company and learn to dance—to apply the skills she has learned over the years, and to use the finely honed tool, her body, she has spent so long acquiring. Suddenly, dancing means a lot more than doing exercises and combinations before a mirror in the confines of a studio: it means moving to unfamiliar music, interpreting a role, miming a story, relating to other dancers, responding to an audience. It means performing, something the student is given few opportunities to do simply because she is not ready. When she is, she learns in the *corps de ballet* to dance a part as a choreographer wants it, to be precise and unselfish, to be a partner of the music, and to communicate different moods and feelings through her dancing. Eventually, she may be given small solo parts of her own to show off her own particular qualities and to allow them to develop further. The dancers we see in the lead roles of a ballet are, with rare exceptions, the highly experienced and mature dancers and performers. They seem to get better and better over the first ten,

sometimes more, years from their first solo appearance. They become more refined in their technique, to be sure, but most of all they learn to embellish it with the dramatic, musical, and personal qualities that make a dancer great.

Great dancers: it is to them we tend to attribute a thoroughly enjoyable and entertaining evening at the ballet. But there are other, unseen forces that determine the quality of a performance. We are apt to forget about them, or at least not think of them, and indeed we are supposed to. But they are things without which, try as the dancers might, there would be no ballet as we know it: choreography, and the many components of what could be called "the dynamics of performance."

CHOREOGRAPHY

Choreography is the making of dances. Its chief aim is to produce something entertaining, pleasurable, even beautiful. Like painting and composing, choreography is primarily an artistic endeavor, a process of creating art for art's sake. Though it has been used for social comment or commercial purposes—just as painting and composing have—it does not really lend itself to such ends, and good choreography does not, as a rule, deal with them.

Good choreography—or, from the audience's point of view, a good ballet—comprises three things, developed in sequence: an underlying concept, or idea; a structure; and steps, or movements. The concept could be something as elaborate as the tale of Sleeping Beauty, but nowadays it is more likely to be what one would term a "theme." The theme could be "love" or some other emotion, an aura or mood such as "the feeling in the air at the park on the first real

spring day," or even a motif such as the "girls all dressed in white" (black, in the original production) of Balanchine's *Concerto Barocco*.

The structure is the overall design (or arrangement or organization) of material. It is what gives a ballet coherence and logical flow—in other words, what allows us to follow it easily, to know who is who and what is going on. All good works of music and literature have such structures: In a novel; the arrangement of episodes in a certain sequence, and then into chapters and perhaps parts, is its structure. In the "Star-Spangled Banner," the structure is to go from the general, even vague ("Oh, say can you see . . . What so proudly we hailed . . .") to the specific and unmistakable ("Oh, say does that star-spangled banner yet wave") in an eight-line stanza of four alternately rhyming lines and two final rhyming couplets. If the episodes of a novel or the lines of the "Star-Spangled Banner" were ordered randomly, the result would be meaningless nonsense. The same is true of ballet. There can be straight, logical progression, as in a simple story. There can be plot within plot, or theme within theme. There can be a theme and variations (Balanchine has named one of his ballets *Theme and Variations*), repeating motifs within a theme, and, carefully done, contrasting themes and motifs, or a sort of point and counterpoint. The permutations—so long as there is order—are almost endless.

The steps of a ballet fit into its structure: Just as a house frame is not built after the interiors are finished, a dance structure is not created around steps. Steps of a ballet may be changed over time—in fact, at least some steps are. The ballet classics and revivals of old ballets seen today certainly do not contain exactly the same steps as the original ballets. Probably any ballet that remains in a company's repertoire for more than a few seasons undergoes changes in steps; sometimes, the choreographer simply forgets some of them, and sometimes he wants to make an improvement. The structure, however, is fixed; were that changed, there would be a different ballet.

The maker of dances—the one who determines the concept, the structure, and the movements—is, of course, the choreographer. Good choreographers, like good ballets, have certain characteristics in common. They have all been fine professional dancers—dancers of above-average, even exceptional technique, and of considerable experience and exposure to ballet tradition. They all have a knowledge of and a feel for music, and some even are musicians in their own right.

But fine technique and musical ability are not enough. If choreography is an art form, then only an artist can choreograph. A virtuoso musician could not compose a fine symphony simply because he is a master technician and gifted performer, and the greatest dancer in the world cannot choreograph simply because he is a great dancer. Mr. Balanchine has said, "If I told fifty well-trained dancers to move, to dance, to entertain me, they would not know what to do." A choreographer must have that intangible, creativity—or artistic genius, or whatever you like to call it. It is the one requirement for his profession that he cannot acquire, no matter how long and hard he studies. He must possess it.

When we think about how most choreographers of quality ballets work, the concept of the choreographer as an artist makes sense. The idea for the ballet is the choreographer's artistic inspiration—springing from a piece of music, or the qualities of a particular dancer, or perhaps some incident or feeling the choreographer has experienced. Like the painter, the choreographer needs his materials to work; he needs his dancers. A good choreographer does not stay home in front of a mirror making a ballet and then call rehearsals to teach it to his dancers; he calls rehearsals first, and then makes the ballet *on* his dancers. By moving at his direction, they keep up his inspiration, they help him work his idea out, they *show* him his idea for his reflection and adjustment. When everything has been arranged the way the choreographer wants it, the dancers embellish it with their own interpretation; they do not violate the music or the actual steps and gestures designed by the choreographer, but they add those touches of personal style and feeling that make a work of art come alive. As one

would expect, the same piece can appear completely different when danced by two different dancers, just as a violin concerto can sound different when played by two different violinists. If there were no room for interpretation—that is, if dancers were rehearsed within an inch of their lives to mechanically do, down to the last expulsion of breath, only what a choreographer directed them to do— the ballet would be flat, lifeless, and stale before it had been seen twice. And it would require only a good technician, not a true dancer, to perform it.

Though the classic choreographic process is simple enough, its importance is enormous, for a ballet developed another way would look unbalanced and wrong. If, for example, a choreographer made up an entire ballet at home and then taught it to his dancers, it would show. It would probably look studiously complex and contrived, and the movements would sit unnaturally on the dancers. If a choreographer worked backward, beginning with the steps—even if he worked from the dancers—the ballet would turn out to be all steps. Because it is not possible to create a structure around steps, the ballet would meander without direction, and the audience would be confused and, ultimately, bored. Unfortunately, some young choreographers take this approach. They make up beautiful steps sometimes, and intricate, interesting ones, but their steps are only combinations that don't add up.

Such ballets may enjoy a period of popularity, but they cannot last. They give themselves away as bad ballets through repeated performance; they expose their own flaws. This is true also of many of the so-called "modern" ballets. Some aspiring choreographers, anxious to win notoriety, use things other than dancing to gain audience approval. They may dress the dancers in brightly colored leotards slashed to the waist, use very loud, popular music, and get everyone onstage jumping around. Tricks pervade, so that much of the performance is similar to an acrobatic display, and sensational techniques, like using an all-male corps in a homoerotic way, are frequently employed. The approach is compa-

rable to using a very sensuous woman to sell paint or Scotch: the woman has nothing to do with the product, but excites the consumer in a positive way. Some modern ballets have nothing to do with ballet dancing, but they excite the audience—at least for a time—in a positive way.

There are more of these "nonballets" and all-steps ballets around than one might think, and with the increase in ballet popularity and the number of aspiring young choreographers, they too are on the increase. Even in very reputable companies such works are occasionally seen as young choreographers are given an opportunity to show their stuff. The trend is having a residual effect— and an extremely dangerous one—on the way some dancers in some areas are being trained, and consequently on the quality of the dancing being presented to much of today's balletgoing public. What is happening is that young dancers are, to some extent, being groomed for the flashy, complex ballet. The learning of the basics of technique is being significantly deemphasized, and instead students are being "drilled" in the spectacular jumps and turns that excite many audiences. This is true particularly for the boys, who frequently can be seen, both in class and onstage, doing work that is way over their heads. Though they may be able to turn without falling, their turning is rough and sloppy, and they are not proficient at doing much else—like walking across the floor, executing combinations of linking movements, or standing still in a simple pose. In the end, these dancers lose, just as the choreographers of the short-lived "pop" ballets lose, and we in the audience lose.

On the other side, of course, is all the brilliant choreography, and all the superb dancing, that exist, for without the good to try to emulate there would not be the bad. Unless they live in the few American cities that attract or house the leading ballet companies of the world (where even the least successful ballet, if not brilliant, is always competent), most people are exposed to a mixture of good and bad work. While what they see may be less sophisticated than what a big-

city audience sees, they need, in a way, to be more sophisticated viewers because they must learn to recognize the real thing—to distinguish among works of uneven quality.

For those in this situation—not having had the advantage of being brought up on top-quality ballet—it will at first be difficult to tell the difference. More and more the trend is toward abstract ballets, with the emphasis on the choreography rather than story or theme; this is largely due to the work of George Balanchine, who has raised choreography to an art form in its own right and freed it, once and for all, from dependence on opera or other elaborate story framework. How do we discriminate between a fine Balanchine ballet of a contemporary style and the modern or pop ballets just described? Mr. Balanchine also has done things such as use an all-male corps; when something is done for sound artistic reasons, rather than merely for effect, how can we tell? Knowing that the level of virtuosity in this country is very high, and that dancers of excellent technique can be seen in every state, how can we know which are demonstrating wonderful talent and ability, and which are attempting to execute movements of a complexity and difficulty far beyond them?

Well, experience is the best teacher, so for a while at least one should go see everything that comes to town, to watch, reflect, feel, and compare. Feeling is probably the biggest part of it—feeling comfortable with the ballet; that it made sense to you; that it seemed to begin and end naturally. It's useful to think, consciously, whether it was pleasant to look at, or whether it gave you a sense of something—of time, or an emotion, or a mood, or a situation. Think about your responses, both emotional and intellectual, and whether they were elicited by choreography and dancing, or by other aspects of the production. Reflect on the elements of the work that stand out in your mind after the performance is over, and the reasons for it. Perhaps it was a particularly elegant and complicated presentation of line that you enjoyed, or a wonderfully light, amusing quality in the steps. Perhaps you were struck by the appropriateness of a piece in relation to the whole, recognizing the features of the dancing that tied them together. When you have reached this point of starting to see the work as an entity rather than a string of dances for different people or even a string of movements, you will find that you are able to make decisions and judgments about what you see with confidence, and to support them. Attend to the ballet unswervingly from the moment the music starts—as much to the quiet, simple, almost stationary parts as to the more buoyant, active ones—and you will have little trouble keeping pace with its logical flow and artistic changes.

Reviews can provide helpful background on companies and new works while you are getting familiar with the form of ballet. Reading them, however, will not speed the process of getting comfortable with your own judgments of what you see, and in some cases may even slow you down if it undermines your confidence in your own reactions. If you do read reviews, remember that popular does not necessarily mean good (nor unpopular, bad). But a good ballet will eventually be popular, and will last, even though it may take time. This has usually been true of great books or pieces of music, and it is equally true of some great ballets: Balanchine's *Four Temperaments*, now widely performed and much loved, was poorly received at first.

Finally, though you should demand coherence and competent dancing from every ballet, keep in mind that there are no formulas or sets of rules for what ballet should be like, or what can or cannot be done, provided it makes artistic sense. One of the great things for the contemporary audience is that ballet is just now, after four hundred years, coming into its own as a separate art form, and therefore entering a great innovative period. A sound creative approach to choreography and a complete technique have been long established and will never be replaced, but they will always be expanded upon. Some of the old ideas about ballet will undoubtedly give way to new, freer interpretations. Some already have: the idea, for example, that the *corps de ballet* is merely a sort of moving scenery, or framework for soloists, is long gone. Instead, we see today in *Sere-*

nade, for instance, that the *corps is* the soloist, is the basis of the ballet, and in *Allegro Brillante* that the boys' work in the *corps* is much more difficult than the soloists'. Once, ballet without a story, luxurious sets and costumes, and a multitudinous cast could not be imagined; now ballet is abstract, pared down to the bone, with as few as two dancers in an entire work. It is, in effect, getting closer to its own being, distilling down to its essence. It is moving closer and closer to music, showing us what we are also hearing. There is an idea, and there is music, and anything goes as long as it works. To make a lot out of a little, without any trappings or tricks—that is what choreography means today, and why it is at the heart of good ballet.

THE DYNAMICS OF
PERFORMANCE

Every performance, even of the same ballet by the same company, is different, and affects the audience differently. Sometimes we leave the theater feeling positively exhilarated, even profoundly moved, by the performances we have just seen. Sometimes we leave disappointed in a dancer or production we have looked forward to seeing for a long time. Occasionally, for reasons that are impossible to pinpoint, we may feel bored, irritated, or a little tense.

This is all only natural. Ballet is not performed by automatons in a bell jar. Ballet dancers are—we sometimes forget—human beings, and their performance represents an interaction between them and other human beings, the audience. Just as a person—be he in the capacity of salesperson, teacher, storyteller, patient, or politician—warms to his subject if his audience is receptive, so the dancer warms to his role for an audience that vibrates interest and enthusiasm. We have all been members of an audience that seemed to be "up"

and, likewise, of an audience that seemed to be dull or restless. Whatever the principal quality the audience projects, the dancers keenly feel it as they wait behind the curtain or step out onstage, and it affects their performance to a considerable degree. Dancers are professionals, and they go out every night intending to give the best performance possible, but there is no doubt that an excited and supportive audience gives them that extra measure of energy, confidence, daring, and drama that makes a performance great. Such an audience is a subtle, peculiar challenge to the professional.

Remarkably, this effect can be true even when a dancer is suffering from illness, painful injury, fatigue, or severe emotional stress. Usually, however, these things exert an unseen influence on the quality of a dancer's performance. I say *unseen* because a dancer hides everything from the audience in his professional dedication to the goal of creating another world, a world in which everything is done with perfect ease and wondrous grace. He hides his problems behind smiles, in costumes over bandages, by steeling nerves and swallowing pain. Though only another trained dancer can discern a dancer's particular problems, the audience nevertheless is affected by them—in the form of dancing that is lackluster or that betrays an underlying weakness or compromise.

Many other factors in a ballet production affect a performance, both for dancer and watcher. The obvious ones are costumes, scenery, and lighting. They contribute to making ballet true theater and, done well, have the power to draw the audience immediately into the mood and action of the ballet. Done badly, of course, they can distract us from the dancing to the extent that we go away disliking the ballet in spite of its many merits, and complaining about long scene changes, too-bright lighting, and inappropriate or ugly costumes.

Good costumes, scenery, and lighting can have similar effects on dancers, helping them get into their parts and become their characters more readily. Problems with these things, however, can have a dramatic effect on a dancer's performance—particularly problems with costumes. Above all a dancer must feel comfortable and have freedom of movement. If the costume is awkward or throws the dancer off balance in movement; if it doesn't fit quite right; if it needs a safety pin in the back, no matter how tiny or invisible to the audience; if, quite simply, it seems ugly to the wearer, it can worry the dancer's entire performance. The shoes, of course, must be perfect.

Less obvious to us because it does not affect us as directly, but much more critical to the quality of the performance, is the music. Indisputably, live music at the ballet is preferable to recorded. It fills the theater and moves both us and the dancers in a way that recorded music cannot; it has a *physical* effect. Because it has a physical effect, though, it can cause problems if a dancer is inexperienced at dancing to a live orchestra. For the years of training the student has moved only to the accompaniment of a pianist (if he has been lucky; many small schools use recorded music for economic reasons), who plays the same snatches of pieces at the same tempo, day in, day out. Later, when a dancer becomes a member of a company, rehearsals are done to recorded music; most companies cannot afford to have even a pianist at all rehearsals. When the dancer suddenly finds himself dancing to an orchestra, therefore, he can be considerably thrown off: the tempos and rests are different, and the dancing will at first be rather rigid. It takes an experienced and musical dancer to make the transition quickly and "go" with the music.

And then there is the conductor. We little think that he is a critical actor in a performance; after all, he is in charge of the orchestra, not the dancers. But to some extent he conducts the dancers as well, and in some ways is even conducted by them. He is, in fact, a very important figure in the ballet production, and his job there is much harder than at the symphony. The conductor must be an intermediary between music and dancers, a sort of overseer of the interests of each. To the music, he has a responsibility to ensure that it is played as it was

intended to be played; that is, as true to the definitive score as possible. This requires the conductor to be attentive to his orchestra and his sheet music, and to himself be a sensitive and accomplished musician.

To the dancer, the conductor has a responsibility to provide certain musical cues, to be aware at every moment of how the dancer is dancing to the music, and in some cases to wait until the dancer is in a certain position or has completed a certain movement before beginning the music. (In *Le Corsaire pas de deux*, for example, during the man's variation, the music does not begin until the dancer is at the zenith of his first jump.) This requires the conductor always to have an eye on the dancers, and to be sensitive to their individual tempos and musicality.

The conductor's job at the ballet, then, is a particularly demanding one—one that, unfortunately, few conductors have the temperament for. According to Sam Kurkjian of Boston Repertory Ballet, "There aren't that many good ballet conductors. . . . Most conductors I have worked with who have not done ballet are almost traumatized [by their first experience], they're hysterical. . . . It used to be, and still is, that one of the great training grounds for conductors was ballet orchestras . . . because if you can do that, you can do anything."

Even a conductor with the temperament to handle ballet, however, could scarcely be said to be in complete control. The conductor's responsibilities still are somewhat at odds with each other; it is not possible to be perfectly true to the music and at the same time perfectly accommodating to the choreography and dancers. Consequently, a balance must be struck, and some give and take must occur between dancer and conductor. Broadly stated, the ideal unspoken contract would run something like: The conductor will provide and take all musical cues required by the choreography, and will allow for subtle variations in tempo among dancers. The dancer, in turn, will dance as much as possible to the music as it is played, and will not force any dramatic changes in the music on the conductor to accommodate his dancing.

Unfortunately, some dancers, rather selfishly, choose to ignore their part of the bargain. With a total disregard for the music, they will take their tempos as slowly as they like so they can hold their balances longer, or whatever. The result is music that is noticeably stretched out of shape, and a disruption of the flow of the overall performance. For the dancer, the moment of selfish display ultimately hurts his own performance as well.

A delicate relationship with subtle influences, that between dancer and conductor, and one that is difficult for most of us to appreciate fully. The crucial importance of a proper stage floor, however, is immediately apparent, and—though a more prosaic concern than the music—can be an equal contributor to the quality of a performance.

The ideal floor for ballet dancing is smooth, tightly joined, level, unfinished pine. It must be smooth and tightly joined so that the feet don't catch anywhere as they are brushed out or pushed along the floor. Because of the precision with which a dancer's body is placed in balances—indeed, because of the "measure" with which every movement is taken—the floor must be absolutely level; the slightest pitch or warping in a stage can throw the dancer off. A pine floor is best because it "gives" or "breathes" with the movement of the dancer, providing greater rebound from jumps and *piqué* movements than any other surface. Finally, and probably most important, it must be unfinished so that it is not slippery. Everything in ballet depends on the ability of the dancer to hold the foot firmly in position on the floor, in a sense to grip it. The dancer must be able to feel the floor beneath him, particularly in turns, and to descend from jumps or step out on *pointe* with confidence. This is impossible if there is so much as a remnant of wax.

The absence of even one of these specifications presents a real danger to a dancer—the danger of serious injury, even of the end of a career, from a fall. It forces him to hold back a little, to dance with a little hesitation and restraint, to be afraid of abandoning himself totally to the dance. The result is a perfor-

mance very different from that the same dancer or group of dancers would give on a good stage. It will be a little stiff; have a flat, too-even pace; perhaps seem unrhythmic. If you have seen a fair amount of ballet, or seen the company before, you will be able to perceive the reluctance in the dancers' manner.

And for most dancers, a bad floor is the rule rather than the exception. Few theater stages were designed with the requirements of dancers in mind. Many are precariously raked to give audiences a better view; many have trapdoors, outlets, and so on for use in theatrical productions (to say nothing of gouges and embedded nails from past productions). Those theaters that do have good floors for ballet are almost without exception new theaters located in major cities. The resident ballet companies of these theaters dance under quite good conditions during their home seasons, but even they spend many months dancing in lesser theaters while on tour. And the dancers of major ballet companies are in the minority. Most dancers are members of touring companies or small regional or civic ballets that have no "home" theater. Their season is done in rented halls—frequently school auditoriums or even old movie houses—or on outdoor plazas. They dance on linoleum, concrete, pressboard—whatever happens to be there. They adjust their dancing accordingly, and do the few things they can to safeguard themselves. Some small companies have portable floors, usually of a type of rubber, that they carry with them and unroll over the existing floor where they dance. Such floors are expensive, both to buy and to transport, and few companies can afford them. All companies carry with them pounds and pounds of rosin like that used on the bows of stringed instruments. This sticky substance is used on the shoes to skid-proof them; if the floor is very slippery, rosin is cracked and spread all over the stage, giving it the dusty look you may have noticed from the audience. Rosin has its benefits, to be sure, but is by no means a panacea, and too much of it can interfere with the dancing. When the floor is really bad, the program, quite simply, is limited to pieces that can be done with relative safety (albeit discomfort); for example, a lively ballet or very classical piece with many big jumps, lifts, and *piqué* movements might be replaced with a slower ballet or demi-character piece of mostly *terre à terre* dancing.

The size of the stage will also affect the quality of a performance. A ballet that has been rehearsed and danced on a large stage can look out of place and distorted on a small stage. Again, the dancers must try to adjust their dancing. Inadequate space backstage and in the wings can interfere with maneuvering props and scenery, and the hot, crowded conditions can make a dancer tense. All is reflected onstage.

Because we can't ever really know what the theater conditions are like, how a certain dancer is feeling on a given night, or what has just gone on backstage, it is usually difficult to define what was wrong with a performance. A dissatisfying performance, however (unless for reasons of genuine technical incompetence or bad production or choreography), should not be blamed on the dancers or company; the circumstances are usually beyond their control. And the moods, worries, indigestion, and other irritations of audience members are not least among them.

Encores

THE TRAINING

*I*t has been argued, and with a good deal of validity, that the only way to appreciate and understand ballet fully is to study it. "Take a class," I tell people who express a desire to know more about what is going on onstage. Though it takes months of training before an adult even begins to realize how very much the technique involves, even one class can show you some basic things about ballet: that it is a strict and exacting technique; that the training is serious and regimented; that it is a considerably intellectual activity (there's a lot to think about at once, and great concentration is essential); and that it is incredibly strenuous and tough on the body. In short, that (despite all appearances) it is hard.

There are roughly only three divisions in the approximately ten-year span of ballet training: elementary, intermediate, and advanced. Promotion is not automatic; each student is evaluated at the end of each year, and promotion may take place earlier or later than the average three-year period. In the elementary

classes the aim is to lay the foundation for the development of the muscles and the elasticity of the ligaments, and to instill in the pupil the basic positions and movements. (The first year or so of the elementary level, therefore, sometimes goes by the name "Fundamentals.") In the intermediate grades combinations of movements are introduced, attention is paid to grace and line, and the necessary power and strength are fully developed. By the time a student is admitted to the higher grades he should have achieved control, strength, and mastery of the basic movements so that he can translate all this into dance.

Ballet class is no fun, and glamour has no part in it. It is a sobering and humbling experience: There is no fooling around, even in children's classes, no laughter, and encouragement and praise are restrained and rare. Rather, complete seriousness, formality, and the most acute criticism (and sometimes humiliation) are the norm.

The atmosphere of most ballet studios contributes to the serious character of the training, almost as if by design. Ballet studios are typically stark, drab, depressing places: a large, bare room of some dirty institutional color; a dusty, dull floor; some harsh overhead lighting; a rickety upright piano in one corner. Floor-to-ceiling mirrors cover one or more walls, and places at the *barre* opposite them are much in demand. Students never simper or fawn into the mirrors, though; instead they frown, squint, perhaps pout. Those mirrors are another teacher, showing you in reflection everything you do wrong, silently saying, "See how awful you look—your hips are not square, your foot is turned in," or any number of things. Once a student knows intellectually how something should be done, the mirrors are an invaluable correction tool.

Correction is an intrinsic, and a rather curious, part of the training. It consists, mainly, of verbal criticism given *during* the performance of a movement, not after. In other words, the student must attempt to correct his position immediately and, it is hoped, to feel the difference between right and wrong as he does so.

Occasionally correction is done by the teacher's actually manipulating the body into the right place—for example, by taking hold of the heel of an extended foot and turning the leg out more and moving it into correct alignment with the hips. Although this is extremely useful to the student concerned, the rest of the class gets nothing out of it. Because the teacher cannot possibly physically correct every student in the few moments an exercise takes, the verbal correction is the most effective. The teacher stands in the middle of the room, rotating to look at everyone, or circulates the room slowly. Corrections are loudly addressed to the person at fault. The result is that every correction, regardless of the intended recipient, is absorbed by every student in the class. If the teacher has said, "Julie, your shoulder is too far forward, and you're twisting that arm," the entire class automatically checks the position of its shoulders. It is a wonderfully economical and fruitful method.

Verbal correction can, however, be severe, and it should be obvious that it can be very embarrassing. By the time a student has reached the intermediate level he is expected to know the basics cold. Consequently, faults that have to do with *correctness*—not quality of execution—are often met with not only impatience but also vitriol. Sometimes the offending student will be made to repeat a movement over and over while the rest of the class looks on and the teacher continues with a barrage of critical remarks. Although in these cases the student eventually is reduced to such a nervous state that he can only do worse and the entire process is counterproductive, I have yet to come across a teacher, no matter how fair and pleasant, who does not do this occasionally. It is then more than any other time that students feel the keenness of the competition most strongly. It is then—when a dancer who is developing well is torn apart for one weak spot—that you realize that if you're going to make it you must do *everything* correctly, and preferably *well*.

Repetition, therefore, is probably the single most important aspect of the training. One could almost say that the underlying premise of the entire technique is

"Practice makes perfect." The theory is that repeating one step eight times is better than doing four steps two times. Scattered movements will not achieve the aim of mastering the basics.

Strangely enough, repetition does not necessarily mean tedium. In ballet there is always farther to go, because perfectly correct technique is only an ideal. Every ballet student knows this: The most advanced student or mature professional dancer can be found intently repeating a simple step in front of the mirror.

Repetition *can* mean exhaustion, however, and certainly frustration. Steps and movements in ballet require thousands of repetitions, not just to do them well, but to do them at all. *Pirouettes*, for example. *Pirouettes* are one of several ballet movements so tricky that a major portion of class time may occasionally be devoted to their practice. The thing about *pirouettes*, like many other elements of the technique, is that once you've learned them there's always a new dimension: another revolution, another position. And then there are the many other types of turns that build on the basic *pirouette* to be learned—again through long, hard repetition.

Repetition is also necessary for developing another crucial quality in a dancer: stamina. Next time you see a dancer do a string of, say, *entrechats* or big jumps in a circle, think about the wind and endurance it takes. When *entrechat* is practiced in class, dancers progress from doing sets of 8 at a time to sets of 16 to 32. Another set or two of the same number of jumps is always repeated after a short breather. For a while those 8 jumps are killing; jumps 5 and 6 begin to show deterioration and by jump 8 feet are dragging on the floor. The second set of 8 is uniformly sloppy. Sometimes it is impossible to finish the set at all. With time, with *practice*, the stamina comes and the number of jumps can be increased. Even dances that do not look strenuous are. The holding power required for poses, extensions, and lifts; the energy required for intricate, nimble movements of the feet—all require stamina. When dancers come out for their bows after a

slow, soft, flowing dance, it is almost a shock to see them sweating and breathing heavily. It may look easy, but it is a great strain.

As a result of the repetition theory, no "dancing" takes place in ballet class; the training is simply year after year of exercises, the same exercises, over and over. Every ballet class all over the world is basically the same. Even across levels, very little changes; in the advanced classes it is simply done longer, or higher, or with beats, or faster. Every exercise in class is done to the right side and to the left, including all jumps and turns, a real demand when you consider that we are all "handed" or "sided" to start with.

Class begins with *pliés* at the *barre* in several positions (usually first, second, fourth, and fifth). *Pliés* are a kind of deep knee bend in a very open position, the body held in a steady, extremely pulled up position, and perfectly centered over the legs. They get the all-important hip, knee, and ankle joints working and warmed up, and are excellent not only for the turnout but also for developing correct posture, tight buttocks, and overall balance and control. After *pliés* comes a number of exercises, presented in a fixed sequence, to further develop turnout, work the foot to achieve a good instep, and develop control, agility, strength, and a good extension (or high leg). In the higher grades the same exercises may be performed on half-toe and done faster and with a greater number of repetitions (say, 32 instead of 8). At the end of the *barre* a few limbering or stretching exercises may be done, and then the class is called out to the center.

The most important of the exercises that follow *pliés* at the *barre* is *tendu*. A *tendu* is simply a stretching of the leg from the hip to the toes, out along the floor to the front, side, or back. The dancer stands still in first or fifth position and moves the leg out only as far as it will go without pulling him off the center of his standing leg. It sounds like nothing, but it is a perfect exercise for developing both strength and flexibility in the entire leg and foot. *Tendus* are done in many forms—for example, with *demi-pliés*, or a flexing of the toes, or at different

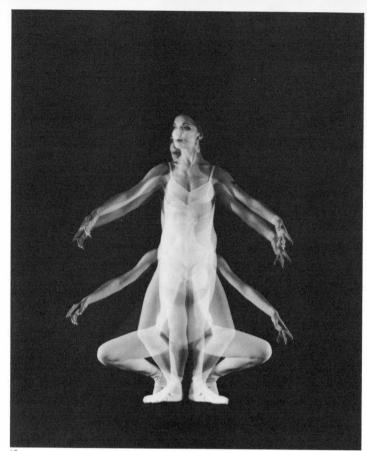

62-65. *Pliés* and *tendus* form the basis of almost all movements in ballet, and so are practiced rigorously at the *barre*. These two pictures of *plié* (one *en face* and one in *effacé*) in first position illustrate how the heels are kept firmly on the floor in *demi-plié*, lifting only when absolutely necessary as the body sinks into the full *plié* . A counterpull of the upper body against the lowering legs keeps the torso erect, and exertion in the buttocks and along the entire inner thigh maintains the turnout.

One can almost see the instep strengthening in the photos of *tendu*, right, as the foot is brushed out along the floor through half-toe to full extension—but without pulling the body off its center. This brushing movement is the same one that begins big jumps such as *grand jeté* and *assemblé*.

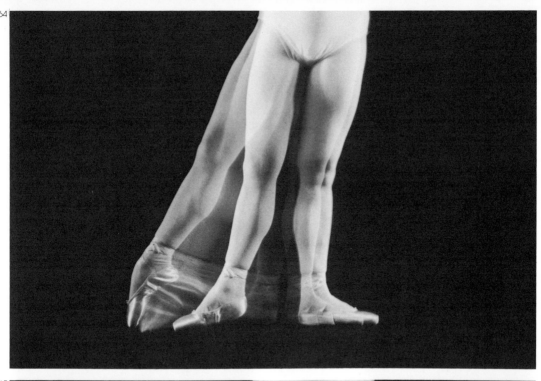

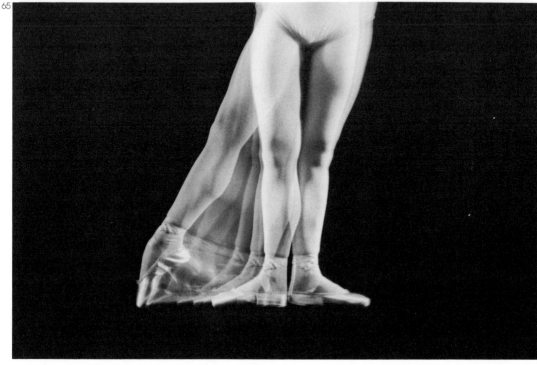

tempos—and several *tendu* exercises will be done in a given class. Whereas too much of some exercises can be harmful, it is virtually impossible to do too many *tendus*.

The exercises in the center consist of the same steps as at the *barre*, only without the *barre* for support. In addition to these exercises, center floor work includes systematic work on the arms, or *port de bras*, and *adagio* and *allegro*. *Adagio* and *allegro* work are combinations, or series of movements, the closest thing to dancing a student ever does. *Adagio* is slow and painstaking and develops grace, line, balance, and sustaining power. *Allegro* is fast and lively, consisting mainly of jumps and rapid turns rather than the more earthbound moves of *adagio*, and is important for lightness, sharpness of movement, and elasticity.

Finally, the students go "across the floor," or "diagonal." Combinations of traveling jumps, turns, and linking movements—e.g., *piqué* turns, *grands jetés*, waltzing, *chaînés*, and *glissades*—are done in this manner. Usually two students perform them at a time, so there is ample opportunity for correction.

At the end of the class the students return to the center, perform the *révérence* (a formal, elaborate curtsy), and applaud and thank the teacher.

The entire class runs about an hour and a half. Throughout, strict discipline and formality reign. Ballet class is not a social occasion. When the teacher enters the studio, the buzzing at the *barre* dies, everyone gets into position, the accompanist sits with hands poised above the keys. Without preliminaries the teacher begins with something like, "*Plié* in all positions, four times, *relevé* and arms up on the fourth. Arms up one, open two." And so it begins, and so it continues. No pleasantries, no jokes: this is business. This is not to say that all ballet teachers are ogres (though some are—dreadful ones), or that teachers never under any circumstances show a sense of humor. It's more as if they realize, from experience, that the only way to learn ballet is to grind away at it, that precision—correctness—is achieved only through hard and regulated work.

THE BALLET TRADITION

*F*or people who have not seen a particular ballet before or who have not been going to the ballet for very long, an evening at the ballet is sometimes discouraging. Some feel overwhelmed—so much goes on onstage at once, and it all moves so fast. Others lose track of the story, and end up focusing on trying to follow the action or to read program notes in the dark. Too often, balletgoers feel that they can't appreciate the dancing; they find themselves anxious for the long classical *pas de deux* to be over, or can't understand the reason for applause when nothing very exciting seems to be happening.

Almost everyone feels these things, to varying degrees, when first starting to go to the ballet. Some conclude that they don't like the ballet, or don't get it, but such conclusions can only be premature. The art of ballet—technique, theme, music, costumes, sets, choreography, everything—has been evolving for

four hundred years. Even (or perhaps especially) the most contemporary, abstract work is deeply steeped in ballet tradition—a tradition embodying so many refinements, subtleties, and characteristics of style, design, and structure that one cannot possibly expect to understand and enjoy it all without some background and experience.

Both are easy to acquire—particularly some background, which you can gain at home and which will increase your enjoyment tremendously. For any nonabstract ballet, familiarity with the story line will save you a great deal of confusion and therefore distraction from the business at hand—the drama and dancing. It will give you a sense of time, scene, and especially character and relationship that will enhance the dramatic action for you.

In general, program notes are insufficient for this purpose. There are several excellent, comprehensive books that summarize the stories of all extant ballets and give important and interesting statistical information: choreographer; composer; premiere date, place, and dancers; famous leads; and so on. Most of these books contain other useful information, such as a glossary, essays on watching ballet and on choreography, or a short history of the ballet; those compiled by choreographers are particularly interesting and informative, and contain valuable personal insights. They are a one-time, indispensable investment for the regular balletgoer.

Another helpful preparation is to listen to the music a few times before seeing the ballet. This is equally true for the long story ballets, in which music is often used to signal character or a change in mood or action, as for abstract ballets. Nearly all ballet music existed before the idea for the ballet (with a few well-known exceptions such as *Nutcracker* and *Giselle*), so in many ways the music is the true foundation of the ballet. You can derive a good deal of pleasure in being familiar enough with the music to appreciate how the choreographer accommodated the dancing to the piece, working its many changes into his story or theme. With Balanchine, increasingly, having some familiarity with the music would be ideal, for many of his newer works are, essentially, abstractions of music—abstractions of the abstract. Whenever possible, listen to the full score rather than excerpted suites or movements, because that's what you'll be hearing when you see the ballet.

Experience of the richness and variety of ballet tradition is gained by seeing as many different kinds of ballets as you can: big, little; lavish, simple; classic, modern; American, foreign; dramatic, abstract. You will then be able to put what you see into context—to look at it from a perspective of history or style or technical advances, to compare it with other ballets you have seen and make your own judgments about what you like, and to understand how that one part fits into the whole of classical ballet. You will see the similarities and cohesive characteristics that run through every ballet, old and new, as well as their differences—and it will all, eventually, make sense to you.

To get you started in this pleasant survey, and to give you a feel for the kinds of things different ballets have to offer, I have provided here discussions of a few representative ballets of different types. The eight discussions really are only a start—barely beginning to penetrate the ballet repertoire—but should help you get in the habit of looking at ballet comprehensively. They attempt to summarize the dancing itself, touching on story line and music only insofar as necessary for reference points. They talk a little about style, technical difficulty, and choreographic innovation, and let you know where in the ballet you can observe a particular jump or turn, where a famous dance sequence occurs, where to see particularly fine instances of partnering, dramatic dance action, and so on. (Keep in mind that every performance is different, and every ballet in the hands of a different choreographer or artistic director will be different. This is particularly true of the classics, which have been changed and revised many times over the years. These summaries are based on specific performances by specific companies, as listed at the top of each summary. The dancing in performances you see may differ anywhere from a little to a great deal from what is written here.)

The ballets discussed here can be informally classified by type. The first three are classics of the Romantic (or just post-Romantic) period—a fairy-tale ballet, *The Sleeping Beauty*; a dramatic ballet with elements of fantasy, *Swan Lake*; and a fantastic ballet with elements of *ballet blanc, Giselle*. The fourth, also classic, is a ballet burlesque with character and demi-character elements, *Petrouchka*. The fifth is a dramatic, almost melodramatic, ballet, *Fall River Legend*, and the sixth is a storyless *ballet blanc, Les Sylphides*. The last two are *pas de deux* that are complete works in themselves. In *Afternoon of a Faun*, the structure and theme dominate; in *Tchaikovsky Pas de Deux*, the dancing and technique do. They richly illustrate the versatility and great creative possibilities of their short, pared-down form.

Half of these eight ballets are full-length classics. No balletgoer should neglect seeing the classics; they are great works of art, and great entertainment—exciting and dramatic. They have elements you will not find in other types of ballets: big ensemble dances, lavish sets and costumes, mimed storytelling, and a blend of pure classical and demi-character dancing. The big ballets are elaborate productions, and you can't possibly appreciate everything that goes on the first time you see one of them, so don't try. The first time you go, have a knowledge of the story and the music, and then be passive, let it act on you, and enjoy it. (Take your example from children, who love the big ballets; they just sit with rapt and open attention—which is the secret to following and understanding them.) The next time you go, you will notice more and more, and naturally will watch with an increasingly critical eye. And you will find that you learn more from these classic ballets than from any others, and that they give you the foundation for enjoying all the rest.

One more thing. In recent years several major ballets have been made into full-length films, and elaborate productions have many of them been. A film of a ballet is very different from the stage production, of course—as different as any movie is from its play, musical, or book original. Go see them if they come

around; they do have their value for the close observation of near-perfect dancing, usually with the finest dancers in the leads, and are often interesting in
themselves just for sheer spectacle and lavishness.

But remember that a ballet film is no substitute for the stage production. It
is flat, and it decides for you what you will see, what will be emphasized. Close-
up camerawork can be too precious or inappropriate, cutting off part of the body
and focusing, say, on the upper body when it would be much better to see the
feet in combination with the arms, or even the whole scene. It is frustrating to
have a cut like this made practically mid-move.

Television productions of ballet are much the same, although somewhat more
intimate and "actual." The "Dance in America" series, as well as several full-
length ballets broadcast by public television stations, serve a purpose and are
greatly appreciated by balletgoers everywhere, but still are not, alas, the real
thing. Only when seeing a ballet live do you get spontaneity, see the unity of
composition formed by the integration of all the dancers onstage, feel the physical closeness of the music and the dancers. So go to the ballet, and enjoy it for
the beautiful visual work of art, and the superb live entertainment, that it is.

THE SLEEPING BEAUTY

Performance: Boston Ballet; Laura Young (Princess Aurora), Elaine Bauer (Lilac Fairy), Woytek Lowski (Prince Florimund), Anamarie Sarazin (Carabosse)
Choreography: After Marius Petipa; staged by Lorenzo Monreal and E. Virginia Williams
Music: Peter Tchaikovsky

*I*n some form or another, the story of the Sleeping Beauty is familiar to almost everyone. This wonderful tale of good and evil, of youth and love and happiness, of fairies and spells and magic kingdoms, was brought to life nearly a century ago in the form of a glittering theatrical ballet by Tchaikovsky and Petipa. The magic not only of the story, but also of the music and choreography, succeeded in boosting the failing health of the ballet in Russia and placing *The Sleeping Beauty* permanently in the favor of the ballet-going public.

The Sleeping Beauty is a classical ballet in a prologue and three acts. It is a showcase for technically difficult dancing, particularly jumps and *pointe* work; indeed, it seems as if the dancers are continually either in the air or on their toes. It is by no means, however, simply a display of dancing. *The Sleeping Beauty* is superb theater, in which mime, acting, costumes, and scenery play indispensable roles. As with *Giselle*, the music takes on special dramatic importance: It identifies certain characters through repeated melodic themes; cues us in to upcoming danger, suspense, romance, or joy throughout the ballet; and creates the mood for every scene. Listen carefully to the overture for changes in intensity and melody; you will recognize them later in the Prologue when the evil fairy

Carabosse and the good Lilac Fairy are introduced, and they will represent these characters throughout.

The Prologue really constitutes an act. The scene is the christening party for the baby Princess Aurora. Members of the court and other guests arrive to see the baby and congratulate the king and queen. Also attending the party are the child's seven fairy godmothers, attended by cavaliers and maids of honor, who enter one by one. The Lilac Fairy, stunning in a purple costume, is carried in sitting high overhead on the fully uplifted arm of her cavalier, as if on an air-borne throne. After her sensational entrance, the group dances together, *bourrée*-ing in three circles, and the fairies and cavaliers dance briefly, leaving the stage as the maids form a line, holding hands, and dance together.

The fairies then return, one by one, to dance before the king and queen. The variation of the first fairy is slow and smooth, full of *attitude* turns and elongated *développés* in *effacé*. The second fairy's dance is very quick and lively, with lots of turns on *pointe* and sharp, hitch-kick jumps known as *temps de flèche*. The third fairy's variation is done almost entirely on *pointe*, with her little *bourrées* and hops accenting the music; she finishes her dance with light butterfly jumps, in which the legs are kicked up behind in rapid sequence like fluttering wings, and a pose in *attitude* front. The fourth fairy's dance is characterized by sharp *passés* and *entrechats*, the fifth's by the unusual quivering movements of her fingers and the sharp turns of her head, and the sixth's by very fast *pas de chat* on *pointe* and *chaîné* turns. The Lilac Fairy returns to do beautiful *développés* that are carried in an arc as she pivots her body from an *effacé* to a *croisé* position, inside *piqué* turns, and then a repeated phrase of two *sissonnes* (jumps from two feet in fifth that land on two feet in fifth, with one leg extended behind while in the air), a *pirouette* landing in fifth, and then a spring up onto *pointes* in the position known as *sous-sus*. The cavaliers and maids finish the entertainment with a light, aerial dance of *pas de chat*, *pirouettes*, and *cabrioles*.

As they finish their dance, there is a loud, ominous noise, and Carabosse, the evil fairy, is pulled onstage in her chariot by her grotesque rodent attendants. In a forceful dance she expresses her furor at not having been invited to the christening, beating the floor with her *pointes* as if stamping her feet in anger. Further angered when, to no avail, the others try to pacify her, she whips around the room in *piqué* turns and *grands jetés*, then spins to the center in fast *chaîné* turns. With a witchy gleam in her eye, she mimes her curse on the child: Aurora will grow up to be a beautiful, beloved princess, but she will prick her finger and die! Once again the fairies try to intercede, flying gracefully toward her, carried in *grands jetés* by their cavaliers, but they are easily repelled by the evil fairy and are carried back through the air in retreat.

But as Carabosse laughs in triumph, the harp sounds and the Lilac Fairy appears. Stepping between Carabosse and the cradle, she holds up her wand and reassures the court that although Aurora will appear to die, she will only have been put to sleep for one hundred years, after which time a handsome prince will wake her with a kiss. Still outwardly arrogant but in effect overpowered, Carabosse falls back and, shaking a threatening fist, is carried away by the ugly rats. First posing in front *croisé attitudes* that are extended into *développés*, the fairies and their cavaliers exit one by one. With a final bow and reassurance to the king and queen, the Lilac Fairy is carried off in a series of gentle split lifts, ending with a lift into an arched position, bending way back, high overhead.

Act 1 is the occasion of Aurora's sixteenth birthday party—and of the casting of Carabosse's evil spell. The party begins with an entertainment by some of the peasants, children, and courtiers of the kingdom. They dance a light, gay waltz, the women passing under horseshoe-shaped garlands held overhead by the men. The men step forward and, holding their garlands high, do two *sissonnes*, *pas de bourrée*, and *entrechats* in a repeating pattern. The dancers weave around the stage in a bouncy sequence of steps and finish with a great bow to the king and queen.

Now arrives the moment that all—particularly the four young foreign princes who have come to court Aurora—have been waiting for. Suddenly Aurora is on-stage, dancing with youthful joy and exuberance to the happy music. She circles the room in spritely *sauts de chat*, *piqués*, and soft, arcing *développés* before going to greet her parents, who present her to her suitors.

The meeting of Aurora and the four princes is the famous "Rose Adagio," one of the most elegant, breathtaking but understated, dances in ballet. One by one the princes come up next to Aurora, who, still a little shy and facing the audience, does a *développé à la seconde* as each prince briefly takes her hand, and then holds the position momentarily as the hand is withdrawn. Aurora then turns to them and, again one by one, the princes come forward to greet her. Standing in *attitude** on *pointe*, she gives the first prince her right hand, and the prince turns her by the hand in a full circle. He releases her hand and, unfaltering in her pose and balance, she curves her arms overhead like a crown as the next prince steps forward to take her hand and promenade her. As the last suitor lets go of her hand, she extends her *attitude* back into a secure, held *arabesque*.

Aurora now dances alone, supported as necessary by one of the princes. Moving across the stage, she steps out into *arabesque*, lowers to a flat foot, and leans way over in *penché*, her hands held sweetly under her chin. Charmed by the princess, the suitors present her with roses; Aurora, moving across the stage in a series of multiple *pirouettes*, accepts one rose after each set. Again she dances alone, doing beautiful *développés* in *écarté*, posing in *attitude* and *arabesque*, holding every position and turning her body in profile to the audience so they may see her lovely poses. The *adagio* ends as it began, with Aurora being promenaded by each prince as she stands in *attitude*. This time, however, she holds her position for an increasingly longer interlude as each prince releases her hand,

*In a Bolshoi performance of this variation, the dancer stood in perfect, unflinching 90-degree *arabesque* throughout. Though not the traditional pose for this dance, it was—being a much more demanding pose to sustain—the most thrilling variation I have ever seen.

and stands at last with perfect equilibrium as if she could do so forever. But suddenly the music ends, and Aurora runs off into the garden.

After the briefest dance by some of Aurora's friends, she returns to dance again. She jumps across the stage on one *pointe* as she traces little circles in the air with her other, then prances back across the stage again to do a series of *pirouettes*, stopping solidly but softly in fourth position. Standing in *piqué arabesque*, she blows kisses to her friends, and then whirls around the stage in a series of *piqué* turns, *grands jetés*, and *chaînés*.

When Aurora returns once more to dance—her stamina never ceasing to amaze—she seems lighter and more energetic than ever. Her dance is full of little beats, perky *pas de chat* and butterfly jumps, lovely back *attitudes*. During her dance, she stops briefly to accept a gift from an old woman who has appeared at the edge of the court. The old woman is Carabosse in disguise, and the present is the fateful spindle. Spinning away in a circle of *grands jetés* with her new present, Aurora pricks her hand and begins to weaken. To allay the fears of her parents, she tries to dance again, but finally collapses to the ground. Enter the evil Carabosse, a whirling, triumphant devil; but the Lilac Fairy appears and calms all, reiterating that Aurora's "death" is only a deep sleep. Sleeping Beauty is lifted and carried off, and as the court disperses, the Lilac Fairy compassionately puts them all to sleep.

The scene of act 2 is a forest; the time, a hundred years later. A royal party, resting from the activity of a hunt, amuse themselves by dancing and playing a game of blindman's buff. Prince Florimund, the host and leader of the hunt, forces himself to participate despite his restless, distracted state of mind. He shows himself as a strong and noble prince in a dance of *cabrioles*, *pirouettes* finishing in *attitude*, and full turns in the air with one leg held in *passé*. When the party goes out again to hunt, however, the prince stays behind alone. He seems melancholy and dissatisfied, and in his dance seems to be reaching out for something.

Suddenly, the Lilac Fairy is before him. Amazed but polite, he bows to her and listens as she tells him of the cause of his unhappiness and of the beautiful sleeping princess. Skeptical, the prince asks to see her, and the Lilac Fairy points with her wand into the trees. A misty vision of Aurora appears for an instant, then vanishes. Immediately taken with her beauty, the prince begs to see more of her. As he beseeches the Lilac Fairy, the many other fairies of the forest come in and dance, and suddenly Aurora appears in their midst.

The prince and princess begin to dance, he turning her slowly, reverently in beautiful *arabesque* and *attitude* positions. At one point in their dance, the prince kneels on one knee and the princess leans over and touches his shoulder in *arabesque*; by turning his body, he turns her in a very pretty and unusual promenade.

As suddenly as she has appeared, however, she leaves him standing alone, and the other fairies begin to dance, forming beautiful groupings. Aurora returns, but this time she dances alone. Her dancing is stronger, more elegant and mature than that of the princess at the birthday party; she is the same beautiful princess, but grown wise and womanly.

Aurora takes her leave once more, and the fairies dance a pleasantly light and brisk dance of *ballonnés, pas de chat,* and *entrechat.* The prince entreats the Lilac Fairy to take him to Aurora, and they set out on the journey to the king's palace. The journey is a very pretty interlude, completed to the accompaniment of soft but intriguing music, and mimed with sweeping, expressive movement of the arms.

The prince and his conductor arrive safely, but just as they are entering the palace Carabosse and her ugly rats burst in, the evil fairy in a bizarre winged costume. The prince and the Lilac Fairy confront Carabosse, and the prince stabs her with his sword. They enter the chamber where Aurora sleeps (on a bed of roses, of course). Gathering her in his arms, the prince kisses her lips, and the fair princess and all the court awake.

Act 3, of course, is the wedding. Besides the courtiers and ladies in waiting, the guests at the wedding are well-known fairy-tale characters: the White Cat and Puss in Boots, Tom Thumb, Little Red Riding Hood and the Wolf, and the Enchanted Princess and the Bluebird. All of the fairies, too, naturally are there.

The entertainment begins with a *pas de trois* by Aurora's brother and two sisters, and then each of the fairy-tale guests performs a *divertissement*. The dance of the White Cat and Puss in Boots is playful and scrappy, full of preening, pawing, prancing—and lots of *pas de chat*!

The Enchanted Princess and the Bluebird dance the brilliant "Bluebird" *pas de deux*, a rather fast *pas de deux* with many suspended jumps and arm and body movements that call up the image of a bird hovering and darting in the air. The enchanted couple enters with fluttering arms and dance together before each does a variation. The Bluebird does *cabrioles* front and back and numerous *entrechats* (both with beats), and full turns in the air, looking altogether like a hummingbird. The princess's dance is very sharp and accented; she poses in *attitude* or *arabesque* and snaps her body around for a change of direction, almost as in a *fouetté*. Hopping on one leg on *pointe*, she moves the other through *développé* front, into *passé*, and into *développé* back, each time beginning the movement with a jump into second position and from there another little jump into a slightly wider second. After her very difficult and interesting dance, the Bluebird rejoins her and together they move across the stage in a series of *pas de chat* and *développé arabesques* before soaring off the stage.

Next Tom Thumb dances a variation of great leaps and *cabrioles*, and then Red Riding Hood and the Wolf perform a little mock chase through the woods. The royal entertainment is over and Aurora and Prince Florimund finally enter and begin the *"Grand Pas de Deux."*

Aurora begins with a *développé* forward, her back to the audience, bending way back with the support of Prince Florimund. From that position, she pivots on *pointe* so that she is in *arabesque* facing the audience—a very smooth, pretty movement. Their movements throughout this dance communicate confidence in themselves and each other, maturity, and graciousness toward their guests. Florimund complements and frames Aurora's every move, holding his arms in the same position as hers as she *pirouettes* or poses in *arabesque*. Aurora shows her trust and admiration for Florimund, time after time finishing multiple *pirouettes* with a fearless dive toward the floor, only to be caught and lifted effortlessly by her prince into the fish (female horizontal and somewhat dipped) position.

To lively, gypsylike music of the tambourine, Prince Florimund does his first variation. He performs full turns in the air, each time landing in a tight fifth and holding perfectly still—something much more difficult than the jump itself. His dance also includes a finishing set of *chaîné* turns across the floor, a step not often seen in male variations.

Next Aurora dances alone, accenting the music of the violin with little beats and *sissonnes* to the side. Her dance becomes very lyrical, and she simply moves with the music with perfect grace and smoothness, making the simplest walking and running steps beautiful to watch.

After more variations by each, in which we see all the brilliant jumps and turns, Aurora and Prince Florimund come back together, and the entire wedding party joins in an exciting—almost wildly so—mazurka, complete with hand clapping. As the royal couple comes together in the center of the stage, lovely and in love, and the Lilac Fairy comes in to make a final blessing and kneels strongly and protectively in front of them, we can't help being caught up in the happiness of the moment. They are somehow all real to us, and we leave the theater feeling that they will live forever—indeed, happily ever after.

SWAN LAKE

Performance: American Ballet Theatre; Cynthia Gregory (Odette/Odile), Fernando Bujones (Siegfried)
Choreography: Ivanov-Petipa; with staging and supplementary choreography by David Blair
Music: Peter Tchaikovsky

Swan Lake is a must-see for anyone who enjoys ballet and wants to learn more about it. *Swan Lake* shows us everything: complicated classical choreography juxtaposed with simple, dancey demi-character; stunning use of the arms; prominent and effective use of the *corps de ballet*; powerful and compellingly believable dramatics in a story of tragedy, romance, and intrigue; and an exciting Tchaikovsky score. It is theatrical ballet at its fullest and most complete and has, I think, an appeal greater even than that of *The Sleeping Beauty*, *Giselle*, or *The Nutcracker*.

The story begins with a picnic in honor of the twenty-first birthday of Prince Siegfried. The happy occasion is celebrated with a spritely waltz by the kingdom's peasants, and the prince himself dances for the company. His variation includes beautiful full inside turns in the air, one leg extended to the side in second position. The arrival of Siegfried's mother is somewhat of a damper to his spirits, however, for she reminds him that he is obligated to choose a wife the next evening at the ball in his honor. She gives her hunt-loving son a magnificent crossbow for a present, but quickly returns to the subject of his marriage.

The prince reflects on his passing youth as the entertainment continues with a *pas de trois* by his friend Benno and two young women. They dance together,

then each does a variation, the first girl doing sharp little *échappés*, *entrechats*, and jumps on *pointe*, and tracing little circles in the air with her leg (*ronds de jambe en l'air*). Benno does a dance of movements similar to those in Siegfried's first variation, and then the other girl comes in for a variation of brisk footwork and lots of *relevé*. The first girl dances again, doing back *cabrioles*, *sauts de basque* in a circle, and *chaîné* turns; Benno dances once more, doing flashy, double-beaten *cabrioles*, and the three finish the *divertissement* together.

After this entertainment, the court young people toast Siegfried's health and begin to dance, couples "walking" gracefully about and weaving in and out in a waltz step. After this dance of dipping, sweeping movements they go off, leaving Siegfried, increasingly more melancholy, alone. He begins a dance expressive of his mood: big, slow *sissonnes* into *arabesque*; *tours jetés* in a circle; slow, deliberate back *attitude* turns and *chaînés*. He poses in beautiful *pliés arabesques*, his right arm bent in across his chest in an attitude of suffering, then steps forward with the back leg into a deep lunge, his left shoulder turned and extended, as if he reaches for something intangible.

The strains of the eerie-wild music that represents the swans, heard first near the end of the overture, float out on the air, and Benno is at Siegfried's side pointing out the flock in the sky. Siegfried determines to pursue them in a hunt and they set off, despite the late hour, into the dark woods.

Act 2 opens with the swan music to the scene of the lake—misty, dark, and mysterious. When the hunting party arrives at the lake and the swans are nowhere in sight, they decide to continue their hunt into the woods. Siegfried, however, has lost heart for the hunt and decides to remain behind.

No sooner is he left alone than he sees a magnificent swan, which suddenly turns into a beautiful girl before his eyes. He watches her from the trees as she walks, takes small *piqués arabesques*, but moves mostly the head and arms, preening, quivering, half-girl, half-bird. Overcome by curiosity, Siegfried emerges from hiding, but the swan-girl flutters in fright. He calms her down and

she tells him in mime that she is a princess who has been cursed by a sorcerer to be a swan by day until such time as a virgin youth swears eternal love to her and marries her.

Siegfried declares that he loves her forever and will marry her, and they are both filled with joy. But at that moment the wicked sorcerer, von Rothbart, appears behind them at the lakeside, gesturing threateningly toward Siegfried. The prince is ready to shoot the wicked magician, but Odette runs to place her body in front of her evil master, knowing that his death also means hers. She *bourrées* frantically on *pointe* back over to Siegfried and leans over him in the famous *arabesque penchée*—leg extended, head down between the arms, wrists crossed and dangling—that is at once tragic and dignified, pathetic and brave. Von Rothbart disappears, and Odette likewise disappears into the forest, Siegfried going after her.

Enter the swans, and we see some beautiful dancing by the *corps de ballet*. They come in doing *emboîtés*, little hopping steps in which the free leg is lifted smartly in a small front *attitude*. They then do *grands jetés* and *pas de chat* in passing lines; *bourrée* forward in the "neutral" position; and then move in two lines to the sides of the stage, posing in *effacé* back and leaning their heads on their arms as if they are resting. The hunters come in and discover their prey, but Siegfried and Odette return in time for Odette to beseech them not to shoot, miming the action of a hunter drawing a bow as she poses in a strong *piqué arabesque*. The hunters, apprised of the real identity of the swans, take their leave, and Odette and Siegfried disappear into the forest once more. The swans dance again to a beautiful waltz, with two coming out for a dance alone while the others stand in two lines in *croisé* with arms crossed before them. Their dance ends with the swans together in an enchanting group, some standing, some kneeling, heads and arms placed in various positions.

Siegfried enters the glade looking for Odette, who then enters from the other side. She *bourrées* out *en face*, eyes straight ahead, arms out to the side like outstretched wings. She glides like a bird on water to the center of the stage, rises slightly and then sinks to the floor with one leg tucked under her, the other stretched to the front, her upper body and arms folding over the extended leg like wings. Siegfried goes to her, raises her, and, to the slow, sadly sweet strains of the violin, they begin their *pas de deux*. Odette *pirouettes* slowly beneath his arm, leans on him in *arabesque penchée*, her head drooping tragically. With the greatest romance and trust, she *développés* forward, leans over the leg for an instant, and then, letting go, falls back into the secure arms of Siegfried. The swans hop across the stage in *arabesque*, entering the pose with a little *fouetté*, and then the lovers resume their dance. Now they begin a series of elegant lifts and *pirouettes* finishing in *arabesque penchée*, everything done slowly and simply to the violin music. Odette hops across the stage in *arabesque*, her arm leading, and Siegfried lifts her into a low, dipping pose. She does more *pirouettes*, her arms working up over her head, finishing them with her back to the audience and leaning way back toward us. There are more lifts and more *pirouettes*, Odette turning slowly on *pointe* with Siegfried's support, her free foot fluttering in *battements battus* (continuous little beats against the ankle), and finishing her *pirouettes* with an extension of her leg to second position. The entire *adagio* is danced with a penetrating romance and pathos and wonderful attentiveness on the part of Siegfried, whose every movement of the arms closely patterns Odette's. Notice how Siegfried almost always holds Odette by the wrists, leaving the hands free for their characteristic tragic, winglike draping.

After this moving *pas de deux*, four swans enter for the famous *corps de ballet* dance, one that always comes to mind at the thought of *Swan Lake*. With crossed arms and joined hands, the swans *emboîté* across the stage and then do a completely winning combination of *échappé*, *relevé passé*, *entrechat*, and *pas de chat*. Throughout, the arms remain joined, requiring the dancers not only to move in perfect unison but also to dance *identically*—one swan with a *pas de chat* a fraction larger than another's, one *échappé* closed an instant more quickly

than another's, and all would be lost. It is a very difficult dance that moreover must be executed with sharpness, speed, and precision. Notice also the constant change in the position of the head in concert, which adds interest and character to a dance that is, rather unusually, done completely *en face*. The dance by the four swan maidens is contrasted by a slower, smoother, but equally joyous dance by two more swans.

Odette returns, doing a variation with *rond de jambe en l'air* brought down into fourth position *croisé*, her arms going up overhead. She does *attitudes* and repeated phrases of two *sissonnes*, a little run, and *développé arabesque*. She moves across the floor in inside *piqué* turns, some of them doubles, changing to *bourrées* and then to *chaînés*. Throughout, her arms pass untiringly through a rich display of characteristic moves.

The swans return, moving across the stage in *ballonné* and hopped *arabesques*, the head in the familiar position down over the arm. Odette comes back, also doing *ballonné* and posing in *arabesque*. The music builds in speed, and with astonishing sharpness and skill at such a fast tempo Odette performs *relevés passés*, *entrechats*, and swift *chaînés* that carry her off the stage. She rushes back into the arms of Siegfried, who has returned to the glade. Day is breaking, and Odette pulls away, physically and emotionally struggling, from Siegfried, her arms fluttering wildly, her back arching away as Siegfried holds her wrists and her *pointes* beat frantically against the ground. She breaks away, her body trembling with emotion as she *bourrées* back toward the lake. Von Rothbart appears behind her and suddenly she is transformed; her quivering body stiffens, her entire being cools, and, eyes straight ahead and arms to the side, she *bourrées* off as she entered at the beginning of the act: facing the audience and as aloof as if she sees and knows nothing.

Act 3 takes place the next evening at the palace, the scene of Siegfried's birthday ball. To the beat of a royal march, guests from many lands arrive. Siegfried and his mother enter last and are treated to a show of native dances by their

guests. First to dance are the Hungarians, who perform a *czardas*, a demi-character dance to a building tempo that uses many classical steps such as *développés* and *pas de bourrée*, but without turnout or classical arms. The Spanish guests dance second, bouncing in a type of *balancé* and deep, accented *pas de bourrée*, and throwing their arms up with characteristic native pride. A Neapolitan dance follows, executed by the Italian guests. The boys do big *ballonnés*, *arabesques* hopped up into *temps de flèche*, and hopping promenades in *attitude* front and back. The entertainment concludes with a lively *mazurka*, couples skipping and running in patterns on the stage and interspersing their steps with quick little kicks of the feet.

Throughout the entertainment Siegfried daydreams of Odette, and the princess mother upbraids her distracted son for being so inattentive to their guests. Siegfried promises not to embarrass her, but even the arrival of the six eligible princesses fails to rouse his interest. In fact, it only serves to plunge him into a deeper reverie about Odette and his pledge of love, and he stares unseeing as the princesses dance before him.

But Siegfried is forced to acknowledge their presence, however slightly, when he dutifully steps forward to dance briefly with each of them. He supports them in *pirouettes* and promenades them in *développés* and a pretty *attitude* that wraps back around his waist. The girls dance with supreme grace, charm, and femininity, but it is all wasted on the love-struck Siegfried. At his mother's urging to select his bride, he is saved from either choosing or refusing any of the girls by the timely sounding of the trumpet in announcement of other guests.

Von Rothbart, disguised as a nobleman, enters with his daughter Odile, disguised as Odette, and introduces her. Siegfried, overjoyed in his complete deception, goes to her, and the famous Black Swan *pas de deux* begins. When the woman in black *développés* to second position and then turns sharply into *arabesque*, her arms going up overhead and then out with the leg with a knifelike movement, we in the audience immediately know that this is not the real Odette.

Her dancing is too bold, too confident, too teasing and alluring to be Odette's; only Siegfried, blinded by love, is fooled. He attends to every move as Odile dances deliberately, following every line of her legs with her arms, even when the leg is extended front. He even fails to see the image of Odette that appears behind him, holding out her hands to him, because the wicked Odile, spying it herself, cleverly distracts him by imitating Odette's adoring, beseeching figure.

When their dance together is over, Siegfried performs a stunning variation of great traveling jumps—jumps that are truly *volés* (flying)—and double *tours en l'air* interspersed with beautifully smooth *attitude* turns. Odile returns, doing double back *attitude* turns, little beats up the leg into *développé*, and *tours à la seconde* to the inside. With dazzling speed and precision, she does a combination of *piqués*, *chaînés*, and *soutenu* turns diagonally across the stage. The prince comes back, leaping into *grands jetés* from which you think he'll never descend, executing full turns in the air that finish in *arabesque* or on one knee. Then Odile walks in and, taking a fleeting but sure preparation, begins the famous thirty-two *fouetté* turns, doing a double on the count of sixteen and four revolutions for the last four counts. Siegfried, not to be outdone, does amazing multiple *tours à la seconde*, and then they begin a playful chase across the stage, Odile hopping backward in *plié arabesque*, rising up onto *pointe* every fourth count and holding her pose in perfect balance.

The relentless virtuosity of the variations, with their feeling of teasing and mounting excitement, builds to a thrilling pitch. The dancers, caught up in the emotion and carried along as on a wave, dance in a way that we are rarely so lucky to see: with *abandon*. The power of the moment, unique in ballet, sweeps the entire audience along with it. The atmosphere in the theater, when that moment is at its most successful, can only be described as wild.

Inevitably, the moment comes to an end. Siegfried swears his love to Odile, and the betrayed Odette appears in the background, revealing to Siegfried his folly and deception. As Odile laughs hideously and her father, von Rothbart, gloats in triumph, the distraught Siegfried collapses to the ground. The scene closes to the music's crashing portents of doom.

Day breaks at the lake, the scene of the last act. The swans, striking simple, appealing poses and forming interesting angles with their arms and heads, look anxiously for Odette's return. She finally appears, grief-stricken, and the swans do their best to comfort her. All is lost, however, for under the conditions of the curse, Odette must now die. She gathers a group of swans around her to hide her from Siegfried and to be with her in her last moments. A storm is brewing, and a great flash of lightning frightens the swans, already fearful and upset at the thought of losing their queen. Siegfried rushes into the glade, going from group to group of swans looking for Odette and at the same time trying to calm them down. The swans around Odette bend down for a moment, and Siegfried discovers her. He begs her forgiveness for his fatal folly, and again swears to her his undying love. The lovers dance tenderly, Siegfried gently lifting and prom-enading Odette, Odette turning softly under his arm. Throughout, the swans move sympathetically in soft *balancés* and *ports de bras* bending back toward the doomed couple. They repeat the now familiar back-hopped *arabesque*, the front arm fluttering. They manage to join in the dance of the lovers, to share their grief, and at the same time to remain respectfully separate.

The lovers' parting is cut short by the appearance of von Rothbart, trium-phant but angry at Odette's lingering past her time. Quivering and trembling, her back arching away as her *pointes* pierce the ground in her struggle, Odette wrenches herself from the prince—much as we saw in act 2, but this time with a desperate finality. She rushes down the line of the swans and plunges into the lake. Siegfried, in his conviction that his love for Odette is synonymous with life for him, swiftly follows her. The triumph of true love destroys forevermore the power of von Rothbart and brings his house down. As his castle crumbles to the ground, von Rothbart sinking with it, the swans raise their arms toward the lake over and over, taking little steps forward. The movement is an expression of re-

lief and triumph at von Rothbart's death coupled with a loving farewell and proud tribute to their queen. It is a simple, quiet, effective ending—and, likewise, use of the *corps de ballet*.

As the day brightens, the swans move off into diagonal lines along the shore in quiet mourning of their queen. A gentle note of hope sounds, and a chariotlike open boat appears on the lake carrying Odette and Siegfried, who have been united in death. The boat crosses the lake, the lovers standing tall with an arm around each other's waist, Odette in particular shining with dignity and love. On the banks, the swans raise their heads proudly toward them. The lovers wave and the swans' arms stir in a final, unspoken farewell.

GISELLE

Performance: American Ballet Theatre (film); Carla Fracci (Giselle), Erik Bruhn (Albrecht), Bruce Marks (Hilarion), Toni Lander (Myrtha)
Choreography: After Jean Coralli and Jules Perrot; staged by David Blair
Music: Adolphe Adam

Giselle, the epitome and great success of the Romantic era of ballet, is probably the best choice for your first time attending a full-length classic ballet. It has remained consistently popular for over one hundred thirty years, for many reasons in addition to its romanticism.

Giselle is one of the great dramatic ballets, requiring the ballerina to be both

dancer and actress to the extent that it has often been called the *Hamlet* of ballet. Giselle's character passes from delicate innocence through madness to worldly (and otherworldly) wisdom and maturity. The choreography accommodates these character changes and it is difficult to say which—the dancing or the acting—enhances the other more. The elements of fantasy and the supernatural, the love story, the portrayal of a small Rhine village, and the costuming also contribute to making *Giselle* true theater.

Not the least reason for *Giselle*'s success is its music. It is one of the few scores written specifically for a ballet, to go with an already existing story; it was, in fact, commissioned for the purpose. The music, therefore, is absolutely fitting (despite accusations that it is quaint and tinkly). It has what is rare in ballet music, dramatic unity, flowing with the story and reflecting all its changes of mood, scene, and personality. What's more, it uses leitmotifs to represent certain characters and feelings. These melodies not only herald appearances for the audience but also establish character identities for recognition later in the ballet.

Several aspects of the choreography itself also make *Giselle* a good ballet to go see if you are relatively unfamiliar with technique. *Giselle* is not a "spectacular" ballet, meant as a showcase for virtuoso jumps and fancy footwork. It is, on the other hand, quite simple, light, and elegant; the pace of the dancing, often done half-time to the music, gives you time to really see what's going on (as well as appreciate the difficulty and control involved in dancing the steps at that speed). It repeats combinations and little dances during the leitmotif phrases, so you are able to see things you missed the first time or put a more critical eye on a certain step, a luxury rare in this intricate art. It juxtaposes pure classical dancing with demi-character, teaching us a lesson in style, and it presents us with many slow, sustained classic steps and positions of the body, almost as if for our study rather than simply our enjoyment.

Giselle is in two acts. The first act takes place in the village and includes the courtship of Giselle and Albrecht, the mad scene, and Giselle's suicide. The sec-

ond act takes place within a forest glade at night; the entire action centers around the Wilis (the mythical spirits of engaged maidens who died before their wedding days) and Albrecht's encounter with them and the spirit of Giselle, now among them. The polar change in scene is dramatic.

Watch closely Giselle's first appearance and her first dance with Albrecht. The music here is a recurrent theme, as are many of Giselle's steps. Her first dance is the embodiment of her personality: light, innocent, tentative and fragile, full of joy and pride in her ability to dance. Note particularly, as she dances for the hiding Albrecht, the slow, double *frappés* with *relevé*, very simple but requiring great control and strength at that speed. After Albrecht declares his love Giselle performs a sprightly dance, done half-time, that is repeated throughout the ballet. She does slow *grands jetés*—from a standing position without any preparation to give her "lift"—landing firmly in *attitude* and unwaveringly holding the position after the jump. There are more *frappés*, big *temps de flèche* in which both legs are kicked high to the front, and bouncy *pas de basque* backward toward the rear of the stage. The lightness of execution here is even more remarkable for the fact that it is danced relatively slowly, putting a greater strain on the body than if there were the momentum of speed.

Throughout the first act there are many such examples of highly controlled dancing that come off looking like carefree skipping around. The steps are so simple, so pure, that many of them are done almost as they are done in class— in isolation, with a strong preparation and finish; holding positions; introducing pauses; and sustaining movements as long as possible. We see Giselle, after the villagers return from the fields and begin dancing, perform fluid *développés à la seconde*, simultaneously rising up on *pointe* and slowly revolving into a back *attitude* turn. These are very beautiful, very difficult moves. Albrecht joins in, doing multiple *entrechats*, a step requiring great force, and then landing absolutely stock-still in *plié*, without the slightest rebound off the floor, before pushing off

again from a dead halt. Giselle ends the dance with perfect *piqué* turns toward downstage center, finishing with a fast, triple-spin *piqué* turn.

When the hunting party comes into the village, we once again see Giselle's theme dance in the little dance she performs for Bathilde, the beautiful lady of the group. The party then retires to Giselle's cottage to rest, and the village boys and girls return again to dance, eventually calling Giselle out to join them. Albrecht comes in and places a crown of flowers on Giselle's head, and she dances a really brilliant, difficult solo that includes double *frappés*, double *attitude* turns, and back *attitude* turns. She hops across the stage on *pointe*, all the while doing *frappés* with the free leg, changing the position of the leg, body, and arms each time. After this most exhausting and shining move, she finishes her dance with *piqué* turns with a change of feet, first turning outside from the right leg, then turning inside from the left leg. Giselle and Albrecht then join the *corps* in an ensemble dance. The *corps* is full of spirit and athleticism, using their arms to set their character and their mood. The arms are very open, welcoming, and peasanty (lots of hands on hips communicate this); the movements are big and strong. Note particularly the arms go up in a ∨ position. This is repeated in the choreography throughout the ballet, but with interestingly different effects: here, simple-hearted warmth and friendliness; among the Wilis in act 2, a kind of mystic power and separateness, which holds a touch of holiness on Giselle in the *pas de deux* near the end.

The gay moments quickly come to an end as Hilarion, the jealous gamekeeper, rushes out and identifies Albrecht as a nobleman. The hunting party is called from the cottage for proof, and it is revealed that Albrecht is engaged to Bathilde. The famous mad scene follows. Giselle, shocked and heartbroken, begins to lose her reason. In a wonderful dramatic exhibition, she goes from rage to sentimental reminiscence to confusion and fear to the crazed passion in which she kills herself with Albrecht's sword. During these moments Giselle again goes through

the steps she first danced with Albrecht, acting out their happy times together. The music is the familiar theme, only this time she dances stumblingly, careeningly. Even this dancing is superb; it requires great strength and true technical judgment to dance steps like a dying person while maintaining just enough of their essence to show us that they are the same ones that were performed so gracefully and correctly before.

The forest at night is the realm of the legendary Wilis. Myrtha, their queen, glides in rapid *bourrées* across the stage, dressed in a long white dress (a waltz-length tutu) and veil. She appears again (her veil removed); poses in a clean, sharp *arabesque*; promenades in that position; and begins to dance. She dances precisely, confidently, superbly—but coldly. She calls forth the Wilis, who emerge with crossed arms in white dresses and veils (the bridal dresses they never had a chance to wear?). She orders them to remove their veils and dance. Their dancing is, like Myrtha's, unemotional, perfect, and automatic. The slow, deliberate dancing gives us a good opportunity to observe some classic positions, particularly several variations of first *arabesque*. A remarkable example of control and balance is to be seen in their *relevés arabesques penchées*: they rise up slowly on *pointe* into *arabesque* and then lean forward, the back in a straight line and the head in line with the arm and the shoulder. The placement in this position is totally different from when *arabesque* is done standing still on a flat foot; in the few seconds the movement comprises, there is an intricate series of adjustments in the muscles and a redistribution of the weight and body parts. Note also throughout the dance of Myrtha and the Wilis the repeated use of the V position of the arms.

Myrtha calls up Giselle from her grave. After being initiated into the Wilis, Giselle does a rather wild dance, which takes her offstage. The other Wilis follow, and the stage is empty when Albrecht enters to visit her grave. As he thinks of her, he has visions of her appearing before him—now darting swiftly by, now passing quickly through his arms, now drifting behind him. Then she comes behind him, touches his shoulders, and does a slow *arabesque penchée*. They begin to dance, Giselle's long tutu giving her an ethereal quality as it flashes out slowly, mystically during big turns and *développés*. Watch Giselle's expressive arms, so much a part of her character, especially as they go up in the ∨ position once more. As Giselle and Albrecht dance offstage, Hilarion, the hunter, rushes in and is suddenly surrounded by the Wilis. He dances a wild, beseeching dance, full of *cabrioles* traveling backward and whipping *chaîné* turns, but they remorselessly cast him into the lake. Albrecht reenters and the Wilis almost entrap him, but Giselle gestures him to the sanctuary of the cross on her grave. Myrtha, infuriated, orders Giselle to dance, which she does, performing a difficult solo in which we can see perfect, slow *développés* into second position, carried back into *arabesque*, and then promenade backward. Myrtha then commands Giselle to dance with Albrecht, and she must obey. They begin the major *pas de deux*, full of sustained lifts and many beautiful *développés en écarté* leaning back in a beautiful line. This part of the dance ends just as their reunion in the forest began that night: with Giselle in first *arabesque* behind the kneeling Albrecht, her hand on his shoulder. Giselle dances alone, then Albrecht, who executes triple *pirouettes* that turn right into back *attitude* turns without a new preparation. Giselle then dances again, her variation this time full of intricate footwork, with sharp, repeated *échappés*, *piqué* turns, and very fast, exhausting, traveling *brisés*. In Albrecht's next solo, watch for the many smooth, quick changes in direction of the body, and the squaring of the body in preparation for many full turns in the air (*tours en l'air*), both single and double. Then Giselle's theme music is heard again and she is once more dancing lightly, with many low *grands jetés* and big linking movements across the stage. Albrecht does endless dozens of *entrechats*, standing firm in the center of the stage as the Wilis dance toward him. It is a little silly, but pure virtuosity and display; note the stretch of the feet, the crossed

and pressing thighs, the deep landings in *demi-plié*—all the things that enable him to jump over and over.

Giselle and Albrecht dance together once more. Albrecht is weakening, exhausted by the merciless Myrtha in her effort to dance him to death. Albrecht falls for the last time, unable to get up. The Wilis, with their backs to the audience, bow toward Giselle's grave—a very interesting effect—and then all *bourrée* off; it is near daybreak and they must go. Dawn approaches as Giselle, alone with Albrecht, bends over and raises him up. She knows she must go, and we can see how she begins to move very stiffly, how her whole body turns of a piece, like a doll, as if the witching hour is now over and she must go back on the shelf—or to her grave. And she fades away, leaving Albrecht sunk upon the ground in despair in the daytime realm of mortals.

The entire *pas de deux*, a very long one, is unique in that the *corps* is present the whole time and even participates—as a moving background, as a containing force for Albrecht and Giselle. It also has none of the traditional formal exits and entrances between solos, thereby preserving the dramatic flow. And it has more feeling than many classic *pas de deux*; it is an expression of emotions and thoughts rather than a mere show of good dancing. This "total" approach to the second act is one of the things that make *Giselle* eminently watchable for everyone in the audience. *Giselle* can be enjoyed on as many or as few levels—technical, dramatic, visual, emotional—as suits the individual, making it a ballet one can see year after year with increasing pleasure.

PETROUCHKA

Performance: American Ballet Theatre; Kirk Peterson (Petrouchka), Rebecca Wright (the Ballerina), Marcos Paredes (the Blackamoor), William Carter (the Charlatan).
Choreography: Michel Fokine
Music: Igor Stravinsky

Petrouchka is regarded as one of the great classics of the modern ballet repertory. Nevertheless, few of the world's ballet companies perform it, and many an avid balletgoer has never seen it. The reason, simply, is that it is a difficult ballet, in every sense, to do well—demanding, tricky, complex, problematical. To begin with, the Stravinsky score cannot be played properly by anything short of a precise, highly experienced orchestra led by a conductor with a flawless sense of timing. The production requires a full company, scores of costumes, several changes of scenery—i.e., it is not cheap. And then there is the ballet itself. About half of it is long crowd scenes, rather loosely choreographed, that put a huge burden on the dancers for their success; they must be rehearsed and polished to the point where they are structurally tight enough not to be dull and rambling, but still loose enough to appear natural and vividly human. The rest of the ballet is the behind-the-scenes life of Petrouchka, the Ballerina, and the Blackamoor. This is central action that must come across as peripheral to the crowd scenes—that must be minimized or dimmed by them—but ultimately as intrinsically more significant. It must be acknowledged intellectually as belonging to the world of the unreal, but felt emotionally as disturbingly real. The dancing, not particularly difficult or classical, must more than anything else be injected with a *quality*—clumsiness, exuber-

ance, despair, coquetry. The character of Petrouchka alone requires a dancer who can go from being strong and energetic to weak and lethargic, from exhilarated to depressed—someone with tremendous stamina, sensitivity, and miming and acting ability. The ostensibly simple roles have, therefore, traditionally been danced by a company's most talented and accomplished dancers.

Petrouchka is a tragicomedy about a puppet with human emotions that only bring him unhappiness and ridicule. Petrouchka's death in the end is glibly and easily explained away to people afraid to believe in the existence of things they don't understand, even when they have seen them with their own eyes, but though his body dies his soul triumphs. The summary of and notes on the ballet in *Balanchine's New Complete Stories of the Great Ballets** are excellent, and I refer you to them. Short of repeating them here, I could not communicate the flavor of the ballet so well.

I can, however, point out one or two interesting things, mostly qualitative, about the dancing. Our first view of Petrouchka, the Ballerina, and the Blackamoor is at a street fair; we see them as the world sees them—as lifeless puppets—while their owner, the Charlatan, makes them dance for the crowd. If you have ever worked a marionette, or even tossed about a rag doll with sewn joints, then you are familiar with the kind of movement the dancers accomplish in this scene. Held up by supports under their arms, the dancers duplicate the string-jointed movement of a puppet with almost uncanny realism. *Nothing* moves but the legs—principally the lower legs; the feet prance and shuffle just off the floor with such quickness and independence of the rest of the body that the dancers seem truly to dangle from the controls of a hidden puppeteer. The stretch and muscle control, particularly in the stomach and spine, and the freedom of movement of the legs in the hip socket required for this scene are tremendous. At one point the puppets break away from their supports and a scuffle ensues over the

---

*George Balanchine and Francis Mason, *Balanchine's New Complete Stories of the Great Ballets* (Garden City, N.Y.: Doubleday, 1977).

Ballerina. Still their movements are mechanical and doll-like, even when they do typically "smooth" movements such as turns, because everything is done to an even tempo with a precise, jerky movement to every count. We clearly see that the way in which a movement is danced in relation to music determines whether the dancing will appear interesting and alive, or flat.

The second scene, which takes place in Petrouchka's drab little box, is a difficult and exhausting one for the portrayer of the title role. Within the span of a few minutes he must mime and dance his way through a range of emotions. We see him in frenetic despair, beating along the walls of his box with speedy movements of the hands and feet, like a bee in a bottle or a fly against a window screen. A moment later he has collapsed, hopeless, to the floor (and believe me, by this point he needs the rest); then before we know it he is up, bounding joyfully toward the ceiling, in expression of his love and happiness at the sight of the Ballerina, who has come into his box. When she leaves in repugnance at his behavior, his mood once again swings to angry despair and, finally, exhaustion and grief.

The dancing of the Blackamoor and the Ballerina in scene 3 is in strict contrast to Petrouchka's. Though they flirt and embrace on the divan, the scene is devoid of emotion and romance. The vain, show-offy dancing of the Ballerina and the stiff, clumsy dancing of the Blackamoor are stereotyped and "stupid."

In the last scene we are abruptly brought back to the "real" world of the townspeople and their holiday. Another strong contrast between the lifelessness of the puppets in the previous scene and human feeling is made through the typical Russian folk dancing done by gypsies, nursemaids, coachmen, and other members of the crowd. Accented by stomping feet and clicking fingers, the dancing includes the typical Russian kicks and jumps done from the deep-knee-bend position. The whirling, energetic dancing goes on until the last group of dancers falls to the ground in mock exhaustion and the revelry is interrupted by the sudden entrance of Petrouchka, being chased by the Blackamoor and the

Ballerina. Large as the crowd is and involved as we have gotten in their celebration, we instantly focus on Petrouchka; the action telescopes in on him. The tragedy and the triumph of the ending is captured in the strident wail of Petrouchka's own music as we see him, large as life on a housetop, shaking his fist at the Charlatan holding his broken, earthly puppet's body in the street below.

FALL RIVER LEGEND

Performance: American Ballet Theatre; Jolinda Menendez (the Accused), Michael Owen (Her Pastor), Lisa Lockwood (Herself as a Child), Sara Maule (Her Mother), Lucia Chase (Her Stepmother), Frank Smith (Her Father)
Choreography: Agnes de Mille
Music: Morton Gould

There are three points about *Fall River Legend* that make it of particular interest to the balletgoer who is trying to see a variety of ballet types and choreographic styles. First, the choreography is by a woman: Agnes de Mille, one of the few women choreographers whose work has had wide and lasting appeal. Second, *Fall River Legend* is in every sense an American ballet: choreographed by an American to music by an American composer about a true incident in American history, Lizzie Borden's slaying of her parents in Fall River, Massachusetts, in 1892. Third, it is a rare example of a ballet that communicates (intentionally or not) a message, a bit of social comment, and does so both successfully and without making it the *raison d'être* of the ballet. I went to

see *Fall River Legend* the first time prepared not to like it, and was not only surprised but impressed by the skillful treatment of such themes as violence, sexual and emotional repression, and loneliness. What in other hands might well have come across as amateurish and pathetic is in de Mille's hands professional and rather beautifully tragic. *Fall River Legend* is excellent theater.

The ballet, in essence a danced play, consists of a prologue and eight scenes. It opens with foreboding music to the scene of the gallows. As the condemned Lizzie (referred to as "the Accused") stands silently at her minister's side, the facts of her case are narrated (the only spoken words in the ballet) and reference is made to Lizzie's happy childhood. The gallows swings around to become part of the framework of Lizzie's house, and scene 1, in which Lizzie relives her childhood, begins. Townspeople pass by, their heads and hands fluttering in conversation, and Lizzie, an observer of her own past, sees herself as a child among them. She joins in their dancing as they circle the stage in pairs, waltzing, skipping, lightly jumping. Reminiscing about happier times, she mirrors the dancing of the little girl who is her former self, but she cannot touch her.

Likewise she cannot touch her mother, who, dressed in gray with a white shawl, dances lovingly with her father. He supports her in *attitude* with the up-lifted leg wrapped around his waist and gently lifts her low off the ground as the two Lizzies dance behind them. The Accused then dances with her mother, then with Herself as a Child, alternating partners, doing *cabrioles* front and back and stepping into *arabesque*, keeping the arms rigidly down at her sides as if to symbolize her separation from these images of the past.

The mother of the Accused has not been well, as evidenced by a fainting spell earlier in the scene, and at the end of this dance she collapses. She is carried into the house and after a time a woman comes out with the news that the mother is dead, and wraps the child in a black cape. A stern spinster among the townspeople, a friend of Lizzie's parents but obviously a figure of fear and hatred for Lizzie, the woman has heretofore interfered considerably in family affairs, and

now takes over completely. The distraught father gives in to her, and the Accused—angry, grief-stricken, and knowing too well what is about to happen—trembles convulsively at the scene before her. As the domineering spinster bends to pick up the mother's fallen shawl, the Accused rushes to her father and leaps to his back, as if to hold him back from the clutches of the horrible woman. But the father is oblivious to her presence, and he lifts the spinster up, the shawl across her shoulders, and carries her across the threshold of his house. The door is closed in the child's face, and she is left disregarded and alone.

Scene 2 begins in tense silence. The father and stepmother sit opposite each other, reading and rocking, with an air of stiff formality. The Accused, now a grown woman and fast becoming a spinster herself, enters and takes a chair between them. They rock in silence until the music begins and the Accused jumps up, unable to bear it any longer, and starts moving restlessly around the house. The cruel stepmother cuts short her every attempt at distraction, and insinuates with every look and gesture that the girl "has problems."

Escaping outside, the Accused meets her minister, a kind young man with more than a charitable interest in her. They dance happily, self-consciously shaking hands at the end. The father, now remade along the lines of the stepmother, comes out looking for Lizzie. He reprimands her for socializing with the minister, and the girl is brought, reluctantly, back into the house.

Inside, the three sit staring and rocking again. Lizzie gets up and returns with an ax, terrifying her stepmother. But she merely goes outside, chops some wood (leaving the ax in a stump), returns to the house with some logs, and sits down again.

With the beginning of scene 3, the music becomes lighthearted and happy, and young couples from the town dance outside the Accused's house. Lizzie comes out to watch, growing lonelier and lonelier. The romantic dance of two lovers during a moment of privacy particularly stings her, and when all the

young people have left she jumps up in a fever of anger, jealousy, and despair. She whips across the stage in rapid *chaîné* turns, coming face to face with the ax in the stump, which brings her to a dead stop. She recoils from it and her horrible thoughts, pressing her arms tight to her sides in every pose in a manner expressive of the tumultuous struggle inside her.

She turns away and Her Pastor is before her. He has come looking for her, and brought her a gift of flowers. They dance briefly, and there is some nice partnering here as the Accused, leaning way back, runs backward in *demi-plié* on *pointe*, supported solicitously by her partner. The Accused's moment of happiness ends when her parents come out looking for her. Staring coldly at her stepdaughter, the stepmother whispers to the minister that Lizzie is insane. This sends the Accused into a fit of rage, and when her parents beckon her to enter the house she hesitates a moment and then bravely defies them for the first time in her life by walking away arm in arm with her friend.

The Accused goes with Her Pastor to a prayer meeting, where everyone is kind to her. In a moment alone together, the Accused and Her Pastor acknowledge their love for each other, and when the congregation returns all join in a spirited square dance. At the end of scene 4, however, the parents once again reclaim Lizzie to their own miserable household; as if in a trance, the girl dumbly follows them home.

Scene 5 opens to the Accused sitting on her doorstep, numb to all around her; her parents sit rocking inside. A door has slammed shut in her mind, and she rises and walks automatically to the chopping block, picks up the ax, and goes inside. Darkness falls on the terror-stricken parents and the emotionless Accused.

The lights come up for scene 6, revealing the bloody horror of the murders on the backdrop. The Accused enters, dressed only in her petticoat, which is stained with blood. In a dream, she meets her true mother, whose comfort and approval she seeks. They dance together affectionately at first, but when the mother sees

the bloodstains she scolds her daughter and slaps her smartly. Having been punished, however, Lizzie is forgiven, and her mother rocks her gently before disappearing.

In scene 7, the townspeople have heard the hideous cries of the victims, and rush through the streets trying to locate their source. They hurry along in pairs, heads down and almost under their outstretched arms, in an attitude of anxiety and fear. Inside the house Lizzie lamely attempts to put the parlor in order, but is overcome by strain and anguish. She rushes outside screaming, running wildly through the crowd to the sounds of doom crashed out by the orchestra. The bloodied ax and mother's white shawl are brought from the house; the Accused, silent now, takes the stained shawl and kisses it. The minister arrives, and as he takes her protectively into his arms, she collapses at his feet.

In scene 8, we have come full circle: the Accused stands with Her Pastor, awaiting her execution by hanging. She thinks back on her life, with all its emptiness and denial, and when it is time for her to go she can only open her arms in relief and eagerness to the hangman's noose. With its fatal tightening she is dead, and free.

LES SYLPHIDES

Performance: Ballet Nacional de Cuba; Josefina Méndez, José Zamorano, Rosario Suárez, Cristina Álvarez
Choreography: Michel Fokine; staged by Alicia Alonso
Music: Frédéric Chopin

In 1832, the premiere of *La Sylphide* with Marie Taglioni began the era of the Romantic ballet. It set the standard for many ballets during the nineteenth century about magical winged creatures dressed in flowing white—the so-called *ballets blancs*, or white ballets. *Les Sylphides* is a twentieth-century interpretation of a *ballet blanc*. It lacks a story, but otherwise evokes the character of the old white ballets: it is classical, dreamy, ephemeral, and dripping with "mood." The Chopin piano music is perfectly harmonious with the style and choreography of the ballet, and as enchanting as the dancers.*

The ballet opens with a tableau of Sylphides, standing with crossed arms in charming groups, in a silvery-blue moonlit wood. In the center three Sylphides surround a young man dressed in a full-sleeved silky white shirt with a bow and a black velvet vest—the only man in the ballet. The tableau breaks, the Sylphides raising their arms and *bourrée*ing to form other pretty groups—some standing, some kneeling, their heads and arms held in various graceful positions. They move across the stage with gently waving arms, pose in *arabesque*, and softly wave their outstretched arms.

---

*For those who would like to listen to it beforehand, the pieces are: *Nocturne, Opus 32, No. 2*; *Waltz, Opus 70, No. 1*; *Mazurka, Opus 33, No. 3*; *Mazurka, Opus 67, No. 3*; *Prelude, Opus 28, No. 7*; *Waltz, Opus 64, No. 2*; and *Waltz, Opus 18, No. 1*.

The group in the center moves, and two girls go off while the remaining couple dances briefly, doing back *cabrioles*, lifts in *arabesque*, lots of little beats, and *grands jetés* and *tours jetés* in a circle. One of the Sylphides comes in for a pretty variation of a small spinning movement of *bourrées* in a circle on one spot, *arabesque*, *pas de chat*, *attitude* and *arabesque* turns, and *sauts arabesques* (jumps in *arabesque*). The couple returns and the Sylphide, supported by her partner, poses in *croisé arabesque*. She brings her leg into *attitude*, at the same time bringing her arm from behind to in front of her head, and her partner promenades her in a half-circle before him, bringing her body around for a *penché* in *effacé*. The principal group then dances together, the Sylphides taking turns dancing with their partner. Throughout the *Nocturne* scene, the dancing is very quiet and light, with everything done close to the floor.

A soft but happy waltz begins, and one of the Sylphides does a repeated combination of *grands jetés*, *balancés*, *attitudes*, *tours jetés*, and *emboîtés** back, interspersed with little beats and double *frappés* with *relevé*. Her variation is followed by that of another Sylphide, this time to a more lively, yet still soft, mazurka. The ballerina does *grands jetés* across the stage and off into the wings, repeating this over and over as the other Sylphides stand in profile, softly waving their arms. The Sylphide comes back once more, doing *relevé arabesque*, *tour jeté*, and a continuous, smooth series of single *attitude* turns. She finishes her variation with springy *relevé arabesques* moved in a circle, first to one direction and then another.

The first mazurka is succeeded by another, this time danced by the *danseur* against the stunning backdrop of the Sylphides. His variation consists of a slow hopping in *arabesque* across the stage, *assemblé*, and *sissonne arabesque*, danced three times and the last time finishing with *entrechats*. The music builds, and he

---

*Emboîté literally translated is "boxed." Each leg is alternately brushed back into an open *sur le cou-de-pied* behind the opposite ankle. As the dancer brushes out, she simultaneously pushes off and hops onto the other leg. All movement is very small and close together, as if done in the confines of a box.

finishes with a series of *tours jetés* and *entrechats*, the Sylphides moving gracefully behind him.

As the *danseur* goes off the stage, the Sylphides gather into flowerlike groups, several girls kneeling like petals around one standing girl. A lovely Sylphide enters and begins to dance soft butterfly steps, excruciatingly slow *piqués développés*, and then a very quick, high *piqué développé* that is almost a *battement*. She takes small *assemblés*, stopping suddenly in fifth position *demi-plié* and leaning over in an attitude of listening; her arms float on the air like feathers. Throughout her dance, the orchestra is playing the overture, or prelude, again as if in anticipation of the romantic *pas de deux* to come.

The Sylphide goes off and returns with the *danseur* to the accompaniment of a lovely waltz. The *corps* too now pairs off, and looks on as the couple begins to dance. Their dance begins slowly with gentle lifts, including one in which the Sylphide does a soft *cabriole* as she is swept up into her partner's arms. The tempo of the music increases somewhat, and the couple moves backward on the stage side by side in a gliding step and back *cabrioles*. The ballerina dances alone for a minute, traveling backward in *passé relevé* and a hopped *plié arabesque*. Reunited with her partner, she takes an *attitude* into *arabesque penchée* and then into an interesting turn in a low *demi-plié* on *pointe* under her partner's arm. Close behind the other, the couple does *chassés* (meaning "chased," in which one foot slides behind the other, displacing it, as in a horse's canter) and *cabrioles* across the stage. As the Sylphide *bourrées* behind him, her partner does quick little steps on a diagonal; the couple continues to hold hands despite the difference in their steps.

For a moment all the dancers disappear from the stage and all is silent; then another waltz begins, and the Sylphides return for a sprightly dance of bouncy *balancés*, fast *bourrées*, and big *battements tombés* (falling forward onto the working leg in *demi-plié*) into *arabesque*. Their dancing is interspersed with solos and dances together by two ballerinas and the *danseur*, one of the ballerinas do-

ing incredibly fast *bourrées* backward in the neutral position, the other doing *arabesque* turns and the little spin we saw earlier, very smooth and with a nice, high *arabesque*. During the solos the *corps* moves gracefully behind, bending their upper bodies sideways. With the last measures of the music, they all rush quietly together and the ballet closes with the same lovely tableau with which it opened.

THE AFTERNOON OF A FAUN

Performance: Boston Repertory Ballet; guest artists Allegra Kent and Jean-Pierre Bonnefous of New York City Ballet
Choreography: Jerome Robbins
Music: Claude Debussy

If you know nothing about this ballet when you go to see it, you may be a little confused and indeed wonder where the title came from. Robbins's contemporary *pas de deux* has replaced the original Nijinsky version (now danced only occasionally as a tribute to Nijinsky or his era), which did have the expected woods and faun; Robbins's does not, but it contains echoes of the Mallarmé poem from which Nijinsky drew his work, and is still danced to the haunting prelude to that poem composed by Claude Debussy. For fullest enjoyment of this lovely piece, which has been popular for over twenty-

five years, you should at the very least read about it in one of the big collections of ballet stories, and ideally read the Mallarmé poem, before you go.

The setting is a ballet studio. At the start of the music, which is dreamy and mysterious, a young man, who has been lying asleep on the floor, wakes and begins to stretch, flexing his feet and arching his back. He stands and looks toward the audience into the imaginary studio mirror that spans the front of the stage. He walks slowly across the stage, adjusting his belt, lazily stretching his body, posing now and then, his eyes always on his reflection in the mirror. After preening himself in this half-interested, half-indifferent way, he curls up on the floor again and complacently falls back to sleep.

A girl in practice dress enters the room, walking proudly on *pointe*, and comes to the center of the stage without seeing the boy, her eyes fixed on her image in the mirror. She does a few *développés*, a few back *attitude* turns, and then walks over to the *barre*. The boy, meanwhile, has woken, and after watching her for a moment stands and walks softly toward and behind her at the *barre*. The girl is doing *grand plié* in fifth position; *passé* with the left foot to the knee; and high, held *développé* out to the side, coolly and critically looking into the mirror. As she lowers the leg from *développé* and begins to sink down into *plié* again, the boy lifts her straight up into the air from behind and they come to the center to dance together before the mirror. She does a *développé* to the front and, supported by him, bends incredibly far back—a precarious position requiring great strength and excellent placement. She poses in a beautiful *attitude* and her partner turns her, the movement ending in a deep *demi-plié*. He lifts her to a sitting position on his shoulder and, looking into the mirror, she tries the effect of slowly swinging her legs, like a child.

Throughout their dance, they never once look at each other—even the music sounds aloof, as if it is hiding from itself. They have tacitly submitted to touch and be touched by each other, but the appeal is in the shapes and patterns they

create, the correctness of their poses, and the achievements of their own bodies. In their movements they seem to approach and then avoid more intimate contact, coming close and then pulling away. At one point they approach each other in graceful lunges; their arms encircle without touching, and the boy lifts his partner into a gentle horizontal position. The girl luxuriates in the feeling of the moment, stretching out her body like a cat. Giving in to the moment as well, the boy lowers her gently onto her knees and, for the first time looking straight at her, kisses her. With a stunned, wondrous, and almost fearful look, the girl quickly rises, backs away with her hand to her cheek, and then walks off as she came in, on *pointe*. The boy—resigned, indifferent, seeking escape?—returns to his place at one end of the studio, and settles down to sleep again.

TCHAIKOVSKY PAS DE DEUX

Performance: New York City Ballet; Patricia McBride, Mikhail Baryshnikov
Choreography: George Balanchine
Music: Peter Tchaikovsky

*M*ost *pas de deux* that are performed as stand-alone pieces—for example, the Black Swan or Don Quixote *pas de deux*—are parts of full-length ballets. They are always welcome, but their enjoyment is based, to some extent, on their association in our minds with a tale, with characters in situations and having emotions we know about, with the image of a scene we can call up before our eyes.

Tchaikovsky Pas de Deux is not part of a full-length ballet; it is a dance for

two offered simply and justifiably on its own, and its popularity is testimony to its pure choreographic appeal and interest. This is a dance that, quite simply, makes us feel good. It makes us smile and want to pat our neighbor on the shoulder. No Black Swan intensity, no Giselle tragic romanticism, no Don Quixote brave love. It is friendly and carefree, the way children are and the way we feel, for tiny spaces of our lives, when we are utterly happy.

Dancers who can do what *Tchaikovsky Pas de Deux* demands of them *ought* to be happy; it means that they are first-rate and can handle pieces that stretch their technical capabilities to the limit. The principal characteristic of the dancing required for the choreography is the epitome of what is meant by *ballon* (bounce). All movements exhibit a light, elastic quality; the jumps in particular are high and springy, with light ascents, extended flights, and soft landings. The turns—and there are loads of them—are sprightly and smooth, and most have a little twist, a little finishing touch, that is out of the ordinary and fun. At the beginning of the piece, for example, the woman finishes *pirouettes* with a smooth transition onto one knee, and the man bends over her in *attitude* from behind, making a lovely frame. There is an exceptionally pretty series of inside *pirouettes* done (by necessity) without a preparation, from *arabesque*. These are done in profile, with the man gently holding the woman's waist from in front rather than behind, his hands already supporting her from her previous movement, a leaning over him in *arabesque*; she, of course, must make a perfectly calculated upward shift of her body for the turns. One other simple touch, almost an inflection, occurs in the man's third variation. He does repeated *tours à la seconde*—Baryshnikov's were sensational—interspersed with a single *temps levé*, or little hop, from the supporting leg that is so quick and smooth (and yet so precisely stretched) that the turns are virtually uninterrupted. There are many other brilliant turns to be seen besides: the famous *fouetté* turns by the woman and virtuoso full turns by the man, plus neat, brisk *emboîté en tournant*, in which the feet are alternately placed against the ankle with each half-turn.

The jumps in *Tchaikovsky Pas de Deux* are equally exciting. In the first male variation there is a stunning movement, almost too quick to distinguish, that looks to be a very high front *cabriole* going right into (without landing) *fouetté*, in which the body is whipped around in the air and lands in *arabesque*. There are also unending suspended *grands jetés* in the second male variation and sharp *brisés* front and back in his fourth variation, before the dancers come together for the finish of the dance.

Unlike the jumps and turns, the lifts in this piece are not spectacular—nothing thrown or dropped, just the fairly traditional lifts in the *grand jeté* and fish positions, and a simple lift in *pas de chat*. They are, of course, very nice, very airy—and provide the appropriate artistic balance that prevents this wonderful ballet from being technically overdone.

LOOKING BACKWARD: EVOLUTION OF THE ART AND TECHNIQUE OF BALLET

This short history of ballet is the last thing in this book for a reason: until one has enough experience or interest in a subject, its history can be deadly dull—even irrelevant. Once you have a frame of reference, you suddenly get curious. You start wondering why, how, when? It becomes exciting, because it means something to you. Unfortunately, ballet history books contain too little of the kind of information the balletgoer is likely to be most interested in—how the form and technique of ballet evolved. What there is on the subject—some of it amusing and surprising as well as interesting—I have summarized here for those who, as I did, wonder where in the world the tradition of classical ballet came from, now that they understand what it is.

Ballet was born in Italy, grew up in France, and matured in Russia, where it has enjoyed such a long period of preeminence that many naturally, though mistakenly, believe it is a Russian product. The prototype ballet, presented in Italy

in 1489 at a marriage feast, was a "ballet-banquet" designed as an entertainment for the wedding guests—a fitting origin, considering that ballet's first objective is to be entertaining. It inspired similar fêtes, at which the serving of each course was done as part of a dance, throughout Europe in the halls of the wealthy. Most notable was the *Ballet Comique de la Reine* given in 1581 in France but under the auspices of an Italian, Catherine de Medici. This modest entertainment lasted from 10:00 P.M. to 3:30 A.M. and cost 3,600,000 francs. Though the lavishness of the spectacle alone is reason enough for the notoriety of this "ballet," it has many other claims to fame. First of all, as ballet-comedy, it used drama *and* dance to communicate a theme (the tale of Circe), and as such was the first modern, integrated, theatrical dance-drama. It boasted the first libretto written for a ballet, by a famous violinist of the time, Belgiojoso (frenchified to Beaujoyeux). By this time, *ballet* was a common term, and Belgiojoso, who understood ballet, called it "a geometrical mixture of many persons dancing together to the harmony of several instruments." Not a bad definition, even today.

In 1588, a priest writing under the name of Thoinot Arbeau published a treatise on contemporary dancing, *Orchésographie*, that laid down the principles, or theory, for the five positions of the feet and for centering the weight of the body over the legs. This work, coupled with the *Ballet Comique de la Reine*, established France as the leader in ballet entertainment and training.

France, however, began to get rather carried away. From the late 1500s until the time of Louis XIV, ballets were mostly *"entrées"* of numerous groups of masked dancers, somewhat similar to the *divertissements* of today. Over the years they became increasingly more informal and unpoetic and gradually veered toward the fantastic and grotesque. It was only with the reign of Louis XIV—his patronage and insistence on using the foremost artists—that ballet became dignified and artistic.

Louis loved the ballet, and appeared himself in many performances from boyhood on (as exalted characters, of course). In 1661, he established the Académie Royale de la Danse and in 1669, the Académie Royale de la Musique, appending a school of dancing to the latter in 1672. This was the origin of the state ballet, and of the institution we know today, after over three hundred years of continuous performance, as the Paris Opéra.

A great deal happened over the next few decades. Ballet passed from the privacy of the royal courts to the public theater; the performances could be characterized primarily as operas with dance parts. Women appeared for the first time onstage in public theaters as professionals; Mademoiselle Lafontaine, who made her debut in 1681, is regarded as the first ballerina. Although most dancing was done *terre à terre*, on a horizontal line, because of the heavy costumes, Pierre Beauchamps, Louis's dancing master and choreographer at the Académie Royale, began to use vertical space, more sophisticated movements of the arms, and elevation. There was a definite technique by then, with the French terms universally used, and Beauchamps added to it by establishing the five positions of the feet and emphasizing turnout and the importance of the *en face* position to the audience.

During the reign of Louis XV, from 1715 to 1774, more and greater technical advances were made. These were in part inspired by Pierre Rameau's *The Dancing Master*, published in 1725, which insisted on turnout, openness, and *lack of constraint* in the body, shoulders, and head. He described *pirouettes*, beats, and *jetés*, giving clear details of arm and torso movements, not merely those of the feet.

The great technical achievements of the period are, of course, associated with the great dancers of the time. In the early 1730s, Marie Camargo introduced the *entrechat quatre* (*entrechat six* was achieved by Louise Lany in 1750), as well as several types of *jeté*, the ever useful linking movement *pas de basque*, and full 90-degree turnout. To do *entrechat*, she adopted a heelless shoe and had her dress shortened to above her calf. It was scandalous, but quickly accepted be-

cause it gave the audience many pleasing new steps. In 1733, Marie Sallé created her own scandal by appearing in London (another big ballet city) with her hair down and only a simple muslin dress over her corset and petticoat. Another exciting new movement, *pirouette à la seconde*, was introduced in 1766 at Stuttgart by Anna Heinel.

The theoretical-philosophical side of ballet also enjoyed an important boost during Louis XV's time. With his publication in 1760 of *Lettres sur la Danse et sur les Ballets*, Jean-Georges Noverre pointed out new and lasting directions the form of ballet would take. In outlining all the laws that should govern the art, he urged reform in costumes (the final discarding of masks, restrictive hoop-skirts, absurd wigs), the restoration of mime as an intrinsic part of the art (a technique so perfect that it would be unobtrusive), and the use of the *corps* in true dancing roles. Noverre was the creator of the independent spectacle of the dance—the *ballet d'action*, devoid of speech and singing. Such ballets would have their own stories and drama, with logical structures and without virtuoso intrusions. There would be control over the choreography.

The effects of Noverre's recommendations were seen before long. The mask was abandoned once and for all in 1773. Tunics became popular as costumes, and because bare legs were not, tights were invented (by the costumier at the Opéra, Maillot, around the time of the French Revolution); this total freeing of the legs contributed significantly to vertical design in choreography. Gluck tried to apply many of Noverre's precepts to opera, and Salvatore Vigano, with his version of *La Fille Mal Gardée* (a ballet still occasionally performed), followed Noverre's advice by using gesture, expression, rhythmic pantomime, and moving plastic groupings.

With the turn of the century, attention once again shifted to technique, and the focal points of the ballet world shifted from France and England back to Italy, and on to Russia. The 1800s also brought one of the greatest periods of creative development in the art form of ballet: the Romantic era.

In terms of technique, it was a time not so much for innovating as for refining and defining. The work of one man in particular, the Italian Carlo Blasis, is responsible for the definition of basic ballet technique as we know it today. In 1820, at the ripe old age of seventeen,* Blasis published the first comprehensive book on dancing technique, *An Elementary Treatise upon the Theory and Practice of the Art of Dancing.* The contents of this book, and of its sequel, *The Code of Terpsichore,* nine years later, remain today the crux of pure ballet tradition. It was Blasis who *insisted* on 90-degree turnout because of the equilibrium and facility of movement to be gained by it, illustrating his entire text with drawings of fully turned-out dancers. He abolished the "loose wrist" of the French school, urged dancers to put "a sort of abandon" in their movements, and demanded that dancers have good line and equal ability to both the left and right sides. He emphasized the importance of *adagio,* calling it the "*ne plus ultra*" of the art and the "touchstone" of the dancer, and encouraging serious students not to be enticed into sacrificing its perfection in favor of the showier but less demanding type of dancing. As director of La Scala (beginning in 1837), he laid down the pattern of training still followed by the student today: a minimum period of eight years, four hours a day, beginning between the ages of eight and twelve, and with a month of rest at the end of each year.

At the same time, technique and teaching methods were being refined in Russia as well. Both Charles Didelot and Marius Petipa left France to teach in Russia at the Imperial Russian Theatre (the exodus of French teachers and choreographers to Russia, where ballet was booming, coupled with the increased popularity of opera during the Jenny Lind rage, was principally responsible for the decline of France's preeminence in the ballet). It was Petipa who first took the position that all dancers, both male and female, should be trained so that they could take the place of the highest virtuoso if necessary. Along with Christian Jo-

*Though most biographers put Blasis's birthdate at 1803, Blasis put his age in this work at twenty-three, and there is a provincial record of his birth dated 1797.

hannson, a teacher from Sweden, he shaped the Russian school. Petipa's style became the Russian style, and it remains today as the model for the Soviet state schools. By the time of Petipa's death in 1910, the Russian dancer was supreme in all the world.

The ballets of the day, the Romantic era, are the "classic" ballets of today: *La Sylphide, Giselle, Coppélia, The Sleeping Beauty, The Nutcracker*, and *Swan Lake*. The ballerinas who appeared in the early Romantic ballets became trend setters and the idols of the world. Among them was Marie Taglioni, whose premiere in *La Sylphide* in 1832 made it *de rigueur* for every dancer to dance on *pointe*, and whose costume of a strapless muslin dress with a tight bodice and a skirt to mid-calf, pink tights, and pink satin slippers became traditional. Taglioni was so popular that at one point she was being paid as much as one hundred pounds a performance. Her performances in Russia helped set the standards there, and one story claims that when she left, a pair of her ballet shoes was bought for two hundred rubles, cooked in a delicate sauce, and eaten by a group of unusually fanatical balletomanes at a memorial dinner in her honor. In addition to Taglioni, there were other virtuoso Italian dancers at that time—Carlotta Grisi, for example, and Pierina Legnani with her thirty-two *fouetté* turns.

The first half of the twentieth century belonged to the Russian ballet dancers, thanks not only to Petipa, but to Enrico Cecchetti, an Italian dancer who went to the Imperial Theatre in St. Petersburg as a dancer in 1887; Michel Fokine, who debuted at the Imperial Theatre in 1898; and Serge Diaghilev, art lover and impresario. These three men were responsible for bringing Russian ballet to the Western world, and for creating and maintaining a new style and approach to ballet that signified a new era for dance. Diaghilev was the mastermind and prime mover. He founded the Ballets Russes in France in 1909 and appointed Fokine his choreographer and Cecchetti his ballet master. He was the creator of the one-act danced dramatic poem, the "ballet-ballet" or short ballet we know

today; his company would perform three a night. Working with the great composers and fine artists of the time, Diaghilev produced some of the most remarkable examples of the unification of music, painting, and dancing the world will ever see. Without a doubt, he had a greater influence on *all* aspects of modern art than anyone else ever has, or probably ever will.

With Diaghilev's support, Fokine was able to realize some of the reforms to ballet that had been rejected by the managers of the Imperial Theatre. He was free to use any music he wanted—not just "ballet" music—and thus began some of the greatest choreographer-composer collaborations of all time (e.g., Fokine-Stravinsky for *Firebird* and *Petrouchka*). He used authentic costumes, not just props and suggestive trims. He was the first to really use the *corps* as part of an expressive whole, not just as decoration. He returned the male dancer, whose importance had radically diminished during the heyday of the Romantic ballerina, to a position of prominence. He got rid of conventional "sign language" gesture, insisting that the whole body must be used, both to dance and express, and thereby making dancing truly interpretive.

As dancing master, Cecchetti kept the technique of the Russian-trained dancers superior and taught the other fine dancers who came into the Ballets Russes. It is fair to say that virtually every famous dancer of the early part of the twentieth century was formed, at least in part, by Cecchetti: Pavlova, Karsavina, Dolin, Lifar, Markova, Nijinsky, and more.

In 1915, Léonide Massine succeeded Fokine as choreographer to Diaghilev. His tenure·marks the beginning of a long period of experimentation in ballet. Choreography moved away from the story or plot as a foundation, and began to concentrate more on creating a mood or atmosphere that expressed an idea. George Balanchine took over as choreographer of the Ballets Russes in 1924, and in 1933 he was invited to set up a dancing academy in the United States that would be on a par with the great Imperial and State schools in Russia. He did so, and more, for the School of American Ballet gave rise to a number of per-

forming companies that evolved, by 1948, into the New York City Ballet, the foremost ballet company in the world. Today, the United States—not Russia, or Italy, or England, or France—is the ballet capital of the world, and with the far-reaching influence of Mr. Balanchine's creative genius, it is likely to remain so for many years to come.

INDEX

(Note: Page numbers in boldface indicate illustrative material)

Académie Royale de la Musique, 177

Achilles tendon, 60, 70

Adagio, 21, 179
exercise, 29

Adam, Adopphe, 152

Afternoon of a Faun, The, 134
discussion of, 170–72

Á la quatrième front and back, **36–37**

Á la seconde, **37**

Allegro, 69, 70, 84
exercise, 29, 130
variations, 44

Allegro Brillante, 112

Alonso, Alicia, 167

Álvarez, Cristina, 167

American Ballet Theatre, 144, 152, 159, 162

Anatomy and Ballet (Sparger), 13*n*.

Arabesque position, 35, 44–48, 54, 72, **77**, 90, 93
arms in, 26, 28, 48
first, second, and third, 45, **46**
muscle control in, 8, 9
penché, **46**, **47**

Arbeau, Thoinot, 176

Arms, the, 24–32, 85
in *arabesque*, 28
communication with, 24–25, **30**
correct position, 27–28
line and, 26
pointe work and, 53
positions of, 28–29, **30**, **31**
training, 26, 27, **30**, **31**, 130

Assemblé, 71, **128**

   soutenu en tournant en dehors, 72

Attitude, **22**, 44, 48–49, **56–57**, 72, 90

   in *effacé*, 38

   front and back, **40**, **41**

Audience, dancer's performance and, 114, 119

Back strength, 70

Balance, **30**, 86, 95, 127

Balancés, 99

   muscle control in, 8–9

Balanchine, George, 84, 99, 106, 107, 110, 111, 132–33, 160, 172, 181–82

Balanchine's New Complete Stories of Great Ballets (Balanchine and Mason), 160

Ballerina in a *pas de deux*, 62–63

Ballet blanc, 134, 167

Ballet Comique de la Reine, 176

Ballet d'action, 178

Ballet Nacional de Cuba, 167

Ballet tradition, 131–74

   Afternoon of a Faun, The, 134, 170–72

   Fall River Legend, 134, 162–66

   Giselle, 59, 132, 152–58

   Les Sylphides, 134, 167–70

   Petrouchka, 134, 159–62

   Sleeping Beauty, The, 25, 59, 134, 136–43

   Swan Lake, 9, 32, 85–86, 92, 144–52

   Tchaikovsky Pas de Deux, 34, 134, 172–74

Ballets Russes, 180, 181

Ballon, 69–70, **74**, **80**, 173

Barre exercise, 23, 26, 29, 52, 70–71, 91, 124, 127–30, **128–29**

plié, 127, **128**

port de bras, 26, 27, 29, **30**, **31**, 35, 130

rond de jambe, 27

   à terre, **15**

   en l'air, **15**

   tendu, 127–30, **128**, **129**

Baryshnikov, Mikhail, 172, 173

Battements battus, 147

Battements tombés, 169

Bauer, Elaine, 136

Beats, 69, 70, 71, **80–81**, 82–84

   en face, 84

   see also Jumps

Beauchamps, Pierre, 177

Belgiojoso, 176

Blair, David, 144, 152

Blasis, Carlo, 179

"Bluebird" *pas de deux*, 59, 143

Body positions, *see* Positions, body

Bolshoi Ballet, 24, 139*n.*

Bonnefous, Jean-Pierre, 170

Books on ballet, 132, 160, 176, 178, 179

Boston Repertory Ballet, 116, 170

Bourrée(s), 54, 55

   pas de, 97

   on *pointe*, 97–98

Brisé, 44, **81**, 82

Bruhn, Erik, 152

Bujones, Fernando, 144

Cabriole, 83

   front and back, **80–81**, 83

Camargo, Marie, 177

Carter, William, 159

Cecchetti, Enrico, 45, 180, 181

Chaîné turns, 54, 60, 92–93, 130

Changements, 59

Changements de pieds on *point*, 55

Character dancing, 25

Chase, Lucia, 162

Chassés, 169

Chopin, Fréderic, 167

Choreography, 53, 55, 84, 105–12, 132–33, 178, 181
    choreographic process, 107–108
    concept, theme, and structure, 105–106, 108
    linking movements and, 96, 97, 98–99
    of "modern" ballets, 108–109, 110

Code of Terpsichore, The (Blasis), 179

Concept of a ballet, 105

Concerto Barocco, Balanchine's, 106

Conductor, 115–17, 159

Coppélia, 180

Coralli, Jean, 152

Corps de ballet, 111–12, 144, 147, 152, 155, 169, 170, 178, 181

Costumes, 114–15, 134, 177–78, 180, 181

Coupé, 97

Croisé positions, 33, 34, **40**, **41**, 44, 48

Dance, 101–19
    choreography, 53, 55, 84, 96, 97, 98–99, 105–12
    dynamics of performance, 113–19

"Dance in America," 135

Dancing Master, The (Rameau), 177

Danseur in a *pas de deux*, 61–63, 84

Debussy, Claude, 170

Demi-character dancing, 25, 134, 144

De Mille, Agnes, 162

Demi-plié, 21, 54, 55, **56–57**, 92, 127, **128**
    jumps and, 70, 71, 72–73, 82
    turns and, 86, **87**, 89, 90, 93, 95

Développé(s), 21, **22**, 23, 44
    à la seconde, 34
    back, **43**
    in *effacé* and *croisé*, 34
    front, **42**
    plié, in *effacé*, 38–39
    relevés, 55

Diaghilev, Serge, 180–81

Didelot, Charles, 179

Divertissements, 55

Dolin, Anton, 181

Dying Swan, The, 32

Écarte positions, 34, **42**, **43**, 44

Échappé, 54

Effacé positions, 33, 34, 35, **36–40**, 48

Elementary Treatise upon the Theory and Practice of the Art of Dancing, An (Blasis), 179

Elevation, 69, **74**

Emboîtes, 146, 168

Encores, 121–82

En dedan (inside) turns, 90

En dehors (outside) turns, 90, 93

En face positions, 33, 84, 177

England, 178
Entrechat, **81**, 82
    quatre, 82, 177
    six, 83, 177
Épaulement, 34–35, 44, 49, 85

Falling, 60, 117
Fall River Legend, 134
    discussion of, 162–66
Feet, *see* Legs and feet
Fifth position of the feet, 17, **18**, **19**, 20, 23
Films of ballets, 134–35
Firebird, 181
First position:
    of the arms, 28, **30**, **31**
    of the feet, 17, **18**
Fokine, Michel, 32, 159, 167, 180, 181
Fonteyn, Dame Margot, 35
Fouetté jump, 45
Fouetté turns, 60, 86, 90, 91, 92, 180
Four Temperaments, Balanchine's, 111
Fourth position of the feet, 17, **18, 19**
Fracci, Carla, 152
France, 175, 176–77, 178, 179, 180, 188
Frappé, 70*n*.

Giovanni de Bologna, 48
Giselle, 59, 132, 134, 144, 180
    discussion of, 152–58
Glissade, 97, 99, 130
Gluck, Christoph, 178
Gould, Morton, 162
Grand battement, 27

Grand batterie, **81**, 83, 84, 98
Grand jeté, 59, 71, 72, 73, **74**, **128**, 130
    dessus en tournant battu, 72
Gregory, Cynthia, 144
Grisi, Carlotta, 180

Head, the, *see Épaulement*
Heinel, Anna, 178
History of ballet, 175–82

Imperial Russian Theatre, 179, 180, 181
Injuries, 60–61, 62, 114
Italy, 175–76, 178–79
Ivanov (choreographer), 144

Jeté, 70
    see also Grand jeté; Tour jeté
Johannson, Christian, 179–80
Jumps, 20, 23, 44, 69–84, **74–79**, 85, **128**, 130
    demi-plié and, 70, 71, 72–73, 82
    muscle control and, 73
    on *pointe*, 59
    see also Beats; *specific jumps, e.g. Grand jeté; Pas de chat; Tour jeté*

Karsavina, Tamara, 181
Kent, Allegra, 170
Kurkjian, Sam, 116

La Bayadère, 193
La Fille Mal Gardée, 178
Lafontaine, Mademoiselle, 177

Lander, Toni, 152
Lany, Louise, 177
La Scala, 179
La Sylphide, 167, 180
Le Corsaire pas de deux, 116
Legnani, Pierina, 180
Legs and feet, 12–23
    in beats, 83–84
    five school positions of the feet, 17, **18–19**, 20, 23, 25, 70
    pointe work and, 50, 51–52, 55, **56–57**, 60
    strength and flexibility of, 12, 20–23, 91–92, 127
    training and, 23, 27, 127, **128–29**
    turnout, *see* turnout
Les Sylphides, 134
    discussion of, 167–70
Lettres sur la Danse et sur les Ballets (Noverre), 178
Lifar, Serge, 181
Lighting, 114
Lind, Jenny, 179
Line, **81**, 124
    arms and, 26
Linking movements, 96–99, 130
Lockwood, Lisa, 162
Louis XIV, King, 176–77
Louis XV, King, 177, 178
Lowski, Woytek, 136

McBride, Patricia, 172
Mallarmé, Stéphane, 170, 171

Markova, Alicia, 181
Marks, Bruce, 152
Mason, Francis, 160*n.*
Massine, Léonide, 181
Maule, Sarah, 162
Medici, Catherine de, 176
Méndez, Josefina, 167
Menendez, Jolinda, 162
Monreal, Lorenzo, 136
Movement, 65–99, 124
    defined, 65
Muscle control, 5–11, 55, 94, 124, 127
    in *arabesque* position, 8, 9
    in a balance, 8–9
    individual muscles, 9
    jumps and, 73
    in *passé*, 9
    "pull and counterpull," 9
    relaxation of muscles, 9–10
    teaching and correction of, 10–11
    torso as center of, 8
Music, 181
    effect on the performance of, 115–17
    familiarizing yourself with, 132–33, 134

New York City Ballet, 170, 172, 182
Nijinsky, Waslaw, 170, 181
Noverre, Jean-Georges, 178
Nutcracker, The, 24, 132, 144, 180

Orchésographie, 176
Owen, Michael, 162

Pantomime, 25, 161, 178, 181

Paredes, Marcos, 159

Paris Opera, 177

Partnering, *see Pas de deux*

Pas de basque, 97

Pas de bourrée, 97

Pas de chat, 44, **78–79**

Pas de deux, 44, 61–63, **78**, 92, 116, 131, 134, 147, 170–74

    jumps and beats in, **78**, 84, 174

    turns in, 86, 91, 173

        pirouettes, 91

Pas de trois, 142, 144–45

Passé, **22**, 90

    muscle control in, 9

Pavlova, Anna, 32, 181

Performance, dynamics of, 113–19

Perrot, Jules, 152

Peterson, Kirk, 159

Petipa, Marius, 136, 144, 179–80

Petite and *grande batterie*, **80**, 83, 84

Petrouchka, 134, 181

    discussion of, 159–62

Piqué, 53–54, **56**

    turns, 54, 90, 92–93, 130

Pirouettes, 54, 90–91, 126

    à la seconde, 178

    turnout and, 14

Placement, 1–63, 92, 94

    body positions and, 34–35

    defined, 1

Plié, 55–59, 71

    développé in *effacé*, **38–39**

    training with, 127, **128**

Plisetskaya, Maya, 24, 26, 35

Pointe class, *see* Training

Pointe work, 9, 21, 23, 50–61, 92, 93, 97–98, 180

    balancing, 1

    with a bent knee, 53, 55–59

    relevé, **15**, 52, 53, 54–55, **56–58**, 59

    risks of injury from, 60–61

    shoes and, 50, 51

    "stepping out" or *piqué*, 53–54, 56–57

    training, 51–52

Port de bras, 26, 27, 29, **30**, **31**, 35, 130

Positions, 124

    of the arms, 28–29, **30**, **31**

    of the body, 33–49, **36–43**

        à la quatrième back, **37**

        à la quatrième front, **36**, **37**

        à la seconde effacé front, **37**

        attitude back, **40**, **41**

        attitude front, **40**, **41**

        attitude in *effacé*, **38**

        croisé back, **40, 41**

        croisé front, **40, 41**

        développé back, **43**

        développé front, **42**

        écarté back, **43**

        écarté front, **42**

        effacé back, **40**

        épaulement and, 34–35, 44

        open *plié développé* in *effacé*, 38–39

    of the feet, five school, 17, **18–19**, 20, 23, 25, 70

Posture, 5–8, **7**, 10, 16, 17, 52, 70, 127

    at rest, 6

Posture *(cont'd)*
    torso as center of muscle control, 8
"Pulling up," 7, 9, 17, 52, 95

Rameau, Pierre, 177
Relevé(s), **15**, 52, 53, 54–55, 59, 83
    développés, 55
    "press," 54–55, **58**
    "spring," 54, **56–57**
Révérence, 130
Reviews of ballets, 111
Robbins, Jerome, 170
"Rolling over," 16, 23
Romeo and Juliet, 55, 59
Rond de jambe, 27
    à terre, **15**
    en l'air, **15**
    fouetté, en tournant, 90
"Rose Adagio," 139
Rosin, 118
Royal Ballet, 55
Royale, 82–83
Russia, 175, 178, 179–80

Sallé, Marie, 178
Sarazin, Anamarie, 136
Saut de basque, **74**, **75**
Saut de chat, **74**, **75**
Scenery, 114, 134
School of American Ballet, 181–82
Second position:
    of the arms, 28, **30**, **31**
    of the feet, 17, **18**
Serenade, 111–12

Shoes, toe, 50, 51, 52, 115, 180
    construction of, 51, 177
"Sickled" feet, 16, 23
Sissonne to the side, 74
Sleeping Beauty, The, 25, 59, 134, 180
    discussion of, 136–43
Smith, Frank, 162
Sous-sus, 54, **56–57**
Sparger, C., 13*n*.
Spotting for turns, 88–89, 93, 95
Stability, 14, 16
Stage floors, 60, 61, 117–19
    ideal, 117
Stamina, 126–27
"Star-Spangled Banner," 106
"Stepping out," *see Piqué*
Steps of a ballet, 106
Storyline of a ballet, 132, 134
Stravinsky, Igor, 159, 181
Structure of a ballet, 106
Stuttgart ballet, 178
Suárez, Rosario, 167
Sur le cou-de-pied, **22**, 70
    pirouette, 90*n*.
Swan Lake, 9, 32, 85–86, 134, 180
    discussion of, 144–52

Taglioni, Marie, 167, 180
Tarantella, 84
Tchaikovsky, Peter, 136, 144, 172
Tchaikovsky Pas de Deux, 34, 134
    discussion of, 172–74
Television productions of ballet, 135
Temps de flèche, 137

Terre à terre dancing, 69, 119, 177
Theme and Variations, Balanchine's, 106
Theme of a ballet, 105–106
Third position:
    of the arms, 29, **30**, **31**
    of the feet, 17, **18**, **19**
Tights, invention of, 178
Torso as center of muscle control, 8
Tour à la seconde, 14, 90, 91–92
Tour jeté, 45, **76–77**
Training, 35, 123–30, 179
    adagio and *allegro,* 29, 130
    advanced, 123, 124, 127
    the arms, 26, 27, 29, **30**, **31**, 130
    barre exercise, *see* Barre exercise
    correction in, 124–**25**
    elementary or fundamentals, 123–24
    intermediate, 123, 124, 125
    for jumps and beats, 70–71, 130
    legs and feet, 23, 27, 127, **128–29**
    linking movements, 130
    for *pointe* work, 51–52
    port de bras, see Port de bras
    repetition as central to, 125–26, 127
    stamina, 126–27
    studios, 124
    for turns, 86, 91, 130
"Traveling" movements, 54, 71
    see also specific movements, e.g. Bourées;
        Piqué turns
Turnout, 12–17, 20, **22**, 179
    development of, **15**, 23, 26, 127, **128**
    turns and, 14

well turned out, 14–16, 52, 70
Turns, 23, 54, 60, 71, 85–95, **87**
    demi-plié and, 86, **87**, 89, 90, 93, 95
    "finish," 90
    landing, 89–90, 94, 95
    preparation for, 17–20, 86–88, **87**, 89, 95
    speed of, 86, 89, 93, 94
    spotting for, 88–89, 93, 95
    springing up, **87**, 88, 89
    stepping out, 88
    training for, 86, 130
    turnout and, 14
    types of, 90–94
    see also individual turns, e.g. Pirouettes;
        Tour à la seconde

United States, 181–82

Vaganova (Russian dancer and teacher), 26
Vigano, Salvatore, 178
Villella, Edward, 84
Volé, see "Traveling" movements

Walking, 54
Waltzing, 130
Williams, E. Virginia, 136
Wright, Rebecca, 159

Young, Laura, 136

Zamorano, José, 167